Panoply of Ghana

A. A. Y. Kyerematen

PANOPLY
OF
GHANA

ORNAMENTAL ART IN GHANAIAN
TRADITION AND CULTURE

FREDERICK A. PRAEGER, *Publisher*
NEW YORK

BOOKS THAT MATTER
*Published in the United States of America in 1964
by Frederick A. Praeger, Inc., Publisher
64 University Place, New York 3, N.Y.*

*Made and Printed in Great Britain
by Jarrold & Sons, Limited, Norwich*

Contents

PREFACE

This book was originally planned for publication in November 1959, to coincide with the visit to Ghana of Her Majesty Queen Elizabeth II, Head of the Commonwealth, which was then expected to take place. I was commissioned in the middle of July of that year by the Ghana Information Services to write the script and captions for the photographs.

It meant being allowed barely two months in which to travel round the country in search of the necessary material and to supervise the photographing of the relevant regalia. There were two consequences to this shortness of time.

The first was that, although I endeavoured to cover a good cross-section of the country, some states had regrettably to be left out, owing to distance and bad weather at the time of my tour. The second was that I have had to rely very heavily on the research I had made in Ashanti independently of and prior to my commission. This is the only reason why the Akans, and particularly the Ashantis, are perhaps mentioned more often in my references and illustrations than any other people.

The burden of my official duties since then has prevented me, unfortunately, from taking advantage of the postponement of going to press to continue my research. I need not, however, be too apologetic about the results of these handicaps, for, if this work does not establish anything, it will at least, I hope, show how similar and historically linked are the various cultural forms found in the different parts of Ghana.

It is relevant to state for the benefit of readers for whom Ghana is a 'foreign' country in more respects than one, that it is divided into the following political or administrative Regions: Eastern Region, Western Region, Central Region and Volta Region on the seaboard; Ashanti and Brong-Ahafo in central Ghana; and Northern Region and Upper Region in the north. The major ethnic groups are the Akans, found in all areas except the Northern and Upper Regions; the Ga-Adangme in the Eastern Region; the Ewes in the Volta Region and a large number of tribes in the Northern and Upper Regions which cannot be classified under any one name.

It would be invidious to mention by name the numerous traditional rulers and other persons whom I have approached, the staff of the Information Services Department, both at the headquarters in Accra and in the Regions, and Regional Commissioners and their staffs; but I hope they will all here accept my grateful thanks and heartfelt appreciation of the hospitality they gave me during my rounds and the invaluable help in one form and another afforded me. I must, however, render my special thanks to Otumfoɔ the Asantehene, Sir Osei Agyeman Prempeh II, by whose permission I was first able to apply myself to this kind of study and whose information on his own regalia provided me with the necessary background in tackling the regalia of other traditional rulers. With the Asantehene must be associated his cousin, Mr Harry Owusu-Ansah.

Special mention must also be made of my thanks to the following persons for help I have received from them in connection with this publication: the Reverend Hugh E. Thomas, Mr G. Alan Walker, Mr F. M. Agyemang and Mr A. C. Denteh.

There are very few publications which have relevance to the subject-matter of this book, but the help I have received from them, particularly those of Dr R. S. Rattray, is considerable and is hereby acknowledged with gratitude.

ACKNOWLEDGEMENT

The publishers are indebted to the Ghana Information Services for permission to reproduce all the illustrations with the following exceptions: p. 27 (foot), p. 45 (top), p. 47 (foot), pp. 50–1, p. 84, p. 98 (foot), p. 99 (centre and foot). These are the copyright of the author in his position as Director of the Ghana National Cultural Centre, Kumasi.

INTRODUCTION

Ghana is best known throughout the world for the spectacular manner in which she gained her independence and by the energetic efforts of her Government and people to meet her educational, social and economic needs. As with other African communities, little is known of her traditional culture, particularly of her art. A study of the regalia of her traditional rulers will, however, reveal that she can be proud of a great cultural heritage.

The *Oxford Dictionary* defines regalia as the insignia of royalty used at coronations and other such occasions. In the context of this book, however, the word covers a much wider range of objects, from the most sacrosanct, such as the Golden Stool of the Ashanti and the Stool of Precious Beads of the Denkyiras, to the near-ludicrous, such as an imported siphon, the aerated water from which not only quenches the chief's thirst but also delights his subjects with the hissing sound it makes.

The regalia include the various forms of Ghanaian traditional crafts: weaving, embroidery, carving, pottery, and works in leather, brass, bronze, silver and gold. Some of these show the imagination and ingenuity of the Ghanaian craftsman and rank among the peaks of art design anywhere, while others are important not for their beauty or dignity but for their historical connections, their social and ritual functions or their symbolic meaning.

For a people who never themselves developed the art of writing, the regalia of Ghanaian chiefs have been of special significance in that they have not been merely symbols of the kingly office but have served as the chronicles of early history and the evidence of traditional religion, cosmology and social organization. I am informed that this is one of the reasons why it has been customary for the regalia to be paraded whenever the chief appears in state at a national festival or durbar, so that all who see them may read, mark and inwardly digest what they stand for.

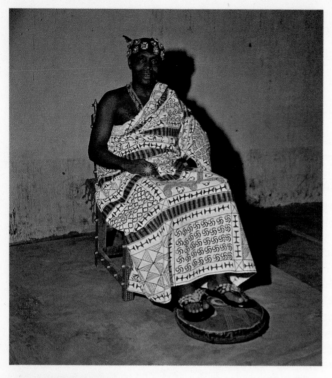

Left Nana Kwafo Akoto II, Akwamuhene, wearing a *kukruboɔ nnwomu* cloth of various *adinkra* patterns such as *nhwemu*, *nkotimsofoɔpuaa* and *donnontoasoo* (from left to right in the bottom piece). The last-named design serves as a border for the whole cloth.

Foot The Navropio, Ruler of the Kasena State*, Navrongo, in a scarlet inner robe, a blue embroidered outer garment and a scarlet cape. This type of costume, showing Islamic influence, is typical of Northern Ghana.

Opposite
Top Otumfoɔ Sir Osei Agyeman Prempeh II, K.B.E., Asantehene, occupant of the Golden Stool and President of the Ashanti House of Chiefs. He is seated on one of his ceremonial chairs, the *ankaahono*, decorated with a gold design of sliced oranges.

Foot The palace of the Wa Na. The architecture, in Western Sudanese Islamic style, is typical of Northern Ghana but unknown in the rest of the country.

* The word "state" in this context and throughout the book refers to what has officially been renamed a "traditional area".

Above
The Ruler of the Akim Abuakwa State, Nana Amoako Atta IV, sitting in state at a durbar and receiving the homage of one of his female subjects. Seated in front of him is one of his *akradwaafɔɔ*, participants in the rites of the purification of his soul.

Opposite
Top Left   The Berekumhene, Nana Akuamoa Boateng II, President of the Brong-Ahafo House of Chiefs, in full regalia.

Bottom Left   The Wa Na, Ruler of the Walas in the north-western corner of Northern Ghana, in ceremonial robes on horseback.

Right   Miafiaga, Togbi Nyaho Tamakloe III, Ruler of the Left Wing Division, the Benkum or Mia of the Anlo State, Volta Region, standing under a coconut tree outside his palace. He wears the *amatsivo* cloth and the *togbenya* cap, popularly used by the Ewes, one of the ethnic groups in Ghana.

Above
Nana Juaben Serwaa III, Ruler of the Juaben State in Ashanti, sitting in state.

Opposite
Top   The Adontenhene of the Akwapim State and Ruler of Aburi, Nana Osae Djan II, riding in a palanquin with his *Ɔkra* seated in front of him. (See p. 92.)

Foot   The smiling Queen Mother of the Mafi State of Tongu, Volta Region, Mama Semama II, wearing strings of precious beads.

Above
Two young girls of the Yilo Krobo State in dresses of precious beads at a 'coming of age' ceremony, called *Dipo*.

Opposite
Top   A durbar scene. The Ruler stands in his palanquin to acknowledge the acclamations of his subjects.

Foot   With the ceremonial state sword a woman swears allegiance to her ruler.

A *lobi* stool from Lawra, Northern Ghana, carried on the left shoulder.

CHAPTER ONE

Stools, Skins and Chairs

STOOLS AND SKINS

The chief emblem of royalty for British and Norwegian monarchs is the crown and for other Scandinavian rulers the bracelet. In Ghana, the stool and the skins of certain animals are the most important of the chief's regalia and the *sine qua non* of his high office. Stools are found among the Akans, the Ewes, the Ga-Adangmes and other tribes of Southern Ghana, i.e. among the Ashanti and in states on the littoral, while skins are used in Northern Ghana.

The reason given for the choice of a stool or a skin as the principal object to betoken the office of a chief is the one-time existence of a special relationship between the people and these articles. This reason may be only conjectural.

For the peoples of the north, who in the past were mostly nomadic and pastoral, a skin was a ready and indispensable possession. The owner would sit or sleep on it during his travels, and, if he was a Moslem, would have daily need of it for his prayers. It was sometimes used as clothing and sometimes to gird a corpse as a loincloth.

Certain animals were thought of as ancestors and a particular animal might be regarded as the *alter ego* of a given person, particularly if his birth or some other event in his life happened to coincide with the appearance of that animal in the village or with some incident connected with it. The skin of that animal would in such an event have a special meaning for that person, and his contact with it was believed to bestow on him the qualities of that animal, the valour and strength of a lion, for example.

Among the settled peoples of the south, the acquisition of a stool was regarded as a prime necessity. The first gift to be made by a father to his child when the latter began to crawl was a stool. Crawling signified that the child had come to stay. A young girl undergoing the rite to mark her attainment of puberty was placed on a stool, and it was customary for a husband to present his newly married wife with a stool to make sure of keeping her. It was on a stool that a deceased person was bathed before being laid in state.

Because of this close association between a person and his stool—there is a saying that there can be no secrets between a man and his stool—it was believed that his spirit inhabited the stool which he regularly used and this persisted even after his death. Hence one was expected, when vacating one's stool, to tilt it on its side, to prevent someone else's spirit or an evil spirit from occupying it.

The skin or the stool thus became stamped with one's personality and it is understandable that it should also be used to mark the position of a chief *vis-à-vis* his subjects. The personality or soul of the personified state or chiefdom was similarly denoted by the skin or stool of the founder of the state or chiefdom, or of the most distinguished of its rulers, or by a special skin or stool believed to have been received miraculously from the Supreme God as a gift.

In Northern Ghana the skin serves as the throne of the chief, the equivalent of the stool in the south. It may be the skin of a goat, sheep, cow, hyena, buffalo, leopard, lion, elephant or kindred mammal. He can sit on any number of these skins at any given time. The *number* of skins used is no indication of his place in the hierarchy of chiefs; but the *type* of skin used is an indication of his status in the state. The fiercer the animal whose skin is used, the more powerful the chief who sits on it is considered to be.

On the skins five cushions are usually placed: one for the seat, one for a back-rest, two for arm-rests, and the fifth as a footstool. The cushions are cased in soft leather with beautifully embroidered appliqué and incised ornaments. The back-rest is placed against a tree or a wall.

Although it appears that some of the royal stools in the south were inspired by domestic stools of the north, for example the Asantehene's *fotoaba* stool which resembles a Bawku stool, there is no tradition, generally speaking, of the stool being used in the north as an item of regalia. An exception, of which I was told by the Bolga Tanga Na, was that among the Frafras the captain of an army went to the battlefield with a stool instead of the usual skins. He was obliged by custom to remain seated on the stool until the enemy or his own troops were routed. From it he gave directions to his men.

Such use of the stool on the battlefield has a parallel in the south. Here the ancestral stools, otherwise called the black stools, were usually taken to the battlefield; if the army was in danger of defeat, the captain would stand on an ancestral stool to give orders to his men to press on. Standing

A ceremonial stool of the Techimanhene, Brong-Ahafo. It is one of the largest stools to be found in Ghana. It is approximately a foot and a half high and the width and length of the seat are about one and a half and two and a half feet respectively. The seat, column and base are all heavily embossed with silver decorations and it has the usual beautifully cast iron bells.

The ceremonial stool of the Afede or Ruler of the Asogli State, Volta Region. It is the principal stool of the state and is regarded as representing the whole state and enshrining its soul. It has power to drive away evil spirits or forces which seek to do harm to the people or their ruler: hence it is called *Zigli*. The smaller stool tied to the central column is a replica of the stool of the founder of the state, Togbi Afede Asor I, and it is that which gives power to the stool. The bar wrapped with charms, touching the two outside legs, gives the power of eloquence to the ruler, the occupant of the stool. The two hooks, one attached to each of the two outside legs, are there to stop thunder. The two bells hanging from the ears of the stool are rung to announce the approach of the ruler. The stool is besmeared with clay and rum whenever it is to be used.

Top A rug, skins and a set of leather cushions with embroidered appliqué and incised decorations, which serve as the throne of the Ya Na, Ruler of the Dagomba State, Northern Ghana.

Foot Two *asipim* chairs of the Akwamuhene, Eastern Region. They are both profusely decorated with ordinary and *mpeaboɔ* brass nails and crowned by *ntuatire* with the eagle's claw motif. The bodies are made of *ɔpepeaa* wood which is resistant against cracks. One of them is decorated with a brass boss both on the back of the chair and the wooden seat. The other has a seat of buffalo skin and the back has a decoration based on the form of a St Andrew's cross. The chairs serve both as ordinary seats in the palace and as seats at State Council meetings.

on the stool was regarded as an abomination, an insult to the ancestors. To avert this, and to prevent the enemy from seizing the stool, the men would brace themselves and fight to the last man. The chief target of an army was the seizure of the captain of the enemy and his ancestral stool.

As regards the use of the skin in the north, it is interesting to note that the most powerful rulers in the south have their stools resting on the skin of a leopard, lion or elephant to denote their strength and power. On certain occasions the Asantehene discards all his richly ornamented stools and chairs and sits on a cushion, *pintaa*, placed on a blanket of coarse northern cloth, *nsaa*, which is spread on the ground. He leans on another cushion propped against a modelled *Nyame Dua* or Tree of God. When this happens, it signifies that the Asantehene is in some distress and is relying on the all-powerful Supreme God for sustenance.

These instances point to a time when the peoples of the north and south may have shared identical cultural institutions or forms; or they may be a reflection of the continuous interchange of ideas and customs between the different ethnic groups of the country in modern times.

Among the stools of chiefs in the south, apart from those used for domestic purposes such as dining (*didi dwa*) and bathing (*Adware dwa*), there are the black stools and the ceremonial stools.

Black stools were originally the special personal stools used by deceased rulers while alive, which on their death were smoked or blackened by being smeared all over with soot mixed with the yolk of an egg. These are preserved in their memory in the stool-house. As already mentioned, it is believed that the spirit of the ruler enters into or saturates his stool even while he is alive and this 'inhabitation' persists after his death.

Black stools, being the abode or shrine of the spirits of the ancestors, became the chief sacramental object and the pivot of the rites connected with the ancestral cult. Ancestors are regarded as lesser gods, and although they are believed to live with and form part of the Being of the Supreme God, it is assumed that they retain in the supernatural world the mode of living to which they were accustomed while on earth. Thus they require food and drink and these are offered them by being placed on their stools on appointed days. In the Dome Division of the Anlo State in the Volta Region the stool-house at Anloga has an annexe with bath and kitchen facilities which is believed to be used by the ancestors when they visit the stool-house.

This feeding of the ancestors is the underlying principle of the various national festivals held throughout Southern Ghana, such as the Adeε, Odwira, Apoɔ, Homowo, Kuntum, Akwammɔ, Tutu, Eguason and Asia-migbe festivals, which are invariably connected with the first harvest or the first catch and also with the custom of pouring libations. Through this feeding and pouring of libations the ancestors are kept in constant touch with their descendants. They punish those who neglect them and do wrong to their neighbours; but also bestow their blessings of peace and prosperity on those who have shown them due respect and lived by the accepted canons of proper behaviour.

The general principle governing the preservation of black stools is that a black stool is preserved in memory of every ruler who succeeds in retaining his office up to the time of his death. But there are exceptions: in certain states there is only one black stool, that of the founder, which represents all successive rulers of the state or chiefdom. An instance is the black stool of the Western Nzima State in the Western Region. This is thought to have been made by Nana Amiherepenin, who is said to have been the first ruler of the Nzima people.

The stool is sometimes not that of the founder of the state but that of the ruler who is regarded as the first to have distinguished himself and fought or worked for the solidarity of the state: for example, the stool of Nana Ohene Gyan, the fourth ruler of the State of Wenchi in the Brong-Ahafo Region. Here the other rulers are commemorated in the royal mausoleum, not in the stool-house, by the unblackened stools used by them during their respective reigns and by a brass casket, the *kuduo*.

At Akropong, the capital of the Akwapim State in the Eastern Region, the state decides which of its rulers should be honoured with black stools; so far only five of its twenty-three rulers have been so honoured, apart from the founder of the state, Nana Ofori Kuma, to whom is dedicated the principal black stool.

The Akwamu State, also in the Eastern Region, has only two stools. One is for the founder, Nana Agyen Kokobo, who led his people from Brong to their first place of settlement further south, Twifo Heman, north of Cape Coast. The other was made by a subsequent ruler, Nana Asare, to commemorate the elder twin brother of the founder of the state who with his supporters chose to remain in Brong. The ruler of the Dormaa State in the Brong-Ahafo Region is held to be the descendant of this twin brother so honoured by the Akwamus. The two black stools are both called *Ampong* and are regarded as two stools in one.

16

Top A ceremonial stool of the Ruler of the Ahanta State in the Western Region with a two-tiered column, the upper one depicting the scene of a chief playing the game of *ware* with his wife, guarded by a sentry holding a gun and entertained to music by a horn player. The lower column has a seated linguist and a state sword-bearer, both holding emblems of their offices, a staff and a sword respectively. They are hidden from full view by a footstool in the form of a tiger having foot-rests on its back. The stool is one of a pair presented to Nana Badoe Bonsu XI by his subjects in recognition of his services to the state. They are used only at the Kuntum festival.

Centre A ceremonial stool of the Ruler of the Buem State in the Volta Region with a column showing two lions, one killing a buffalo and the other holding a chameleon by one of the forelegs and showing it the way with an oil lamp. The buffalo, it is said, boasted that it was as powerful as the lion and so was being humbled. The chameleon that had shown humility was being shown the way to escape.

Foot A ceremonial stool of the Queen Mother of the Peki State, Volta Region, Madame Rosina Nyangomagu.

In the Assin Attandaso State there are two black stools, one for the founder of the state, Nana T'sibu Panyin, and the other, a smaller one, for the first queen mother of the state, Nana Ekuani.

In the stool-room the black stool or stools are placed on beds, skins or wooden platforms and arranged in a straight line or horse-shoe formation. In front of them may be utensils used for feeding the ancestors they represent and also certain articles associated with these ancestors while they were alive. These are usually swords or other military weapons, and musical instruments used by the ruler on the battlefield or in directing his people during their migrations. There are also to be found offerings made to the ancestors by private individuals seeking their help.

The black stool of Togbi Afedi Asor I, the founder of the Asogli State in Ho, Volta Region, for example, has in front of it the sword which the founder used in breaking through the walls of Nɔtsie, whence he led his people to escape the cruelty of a tyrant ruler. There is also a horn.

In front of the Aburam black stool of the Buem State at Borada are three swords, a torch, a case containing poisoned arrows, a short horn and a drum. The arrows are alleged to have been used by Nana Aburam when he led his people from Wenchi in Brong to Kolangbange in the Volta Region. The torch provided light. The short horn sounded, '*M'ani wɔ ko so dabaa dabaa*' ('I am always on my guard against any assailant'). The drum responded, '*Kantamanto*' ('What I swear I never recant').

One or more sacral bells of cast-iron or brass are usually attached to the stool with leather thongs. Some of these are cast locally and others are imported. They are rung when the stools are being carried in a procession. Also attached to the stool may be the skull and leg- or jaw-bones of a defeated enemy warrior, or metal casts thereof.

Most black stools were originally made of *sɛsɛ* wood (*Funtumia africana*) and are usually plain, without ornaments; but those of the Asantehene, the Akwamuhene, and possibly others, have embossed gold-leaf decorations. On most of the ornamented black stools these decorations are unfortunately hidden under an incrustation of the dried blood of sheep sacrificed to the stools. The fat of the sacrificed sheep is placed on a column supporting the seat and base of the stool.

The black stool is regarded not only as a memorial to a deceased successful ruler and a shrine for the soul of the people but is also believed to possess magical powers and to be able to protect and satisfy the needs of the people, by itself, not through the ancestors. The *Amankamdwa* or Stool of Precious

18

Top The eight black stools of the Akim Abuakwa State, Eastern Region, the first from the right and the oldest being called *Okusukrunku*. Each of the stools has its own cup and dish used for the pouring of libations and the feeding of the ancestors. Standing behind the stools are their custodians.

Foot An annexe to the stool-house of the Head of the Dome or Adonten Division of the Anlo State, Anloga, Volta Region, with bath and kitchen facilities for the ancestors.

19

Top A large *asipim* chair with a foot-rest, belonging to the Techimanhene, Brong-Ahafo. They are both richly adorned with ordinary and *mpeaboɔ* brass nails. The back has a *kontonkurowi* circular design and is surmounted by *ntuatire* of stylized eagle's claws. The seat also has the *kontonkurowi* design.

Foot An ornate *asipim* chair with a back designed like that of a *nnamu* or *akonkromfi* armchair. The main design consists of a pair of stylized ram's horns facing each other, *dwennimmɛn ntoasoɔ*. They are a symbol of strength. The chair is also decorated with *mpeaboɔ* brass nails and *ntuatire* of the eagle's claw design. It belongs to the Agogohene of Ashanti-Akim.

20

Beads of the Denkyiras is believed to call down a whirlwind when moved without the performance of the appropriate customary rites.

The origins of such beliefs become obvious from the accounts given of how some of the stools were made. For instance, the column of the Agbaa Stool, the black stool of Maja, the founder of the Manya Krobo State, is said to contain a charm, *kuku*, which is made up in three parts of wood, stone and the flesh of an animal. The black stool of the Effutu State in Winneba, Central Region, is alleged to derive its power from the deer which is sacrificed every four months to the god Penkye Otu.

The reverence and the awe which the people have for their black stools is perhaps best illustrated by the attitude of the Ashanti to the Golden Stool, which is regarded as one of the Asantehene's black stools and represents their ruler Nana Osei Tutu, in whose reign the stool was received, and his immediate successor, Nana Opoku Ware. It is regarded as a living being and so is called *Sikadwa Kofi*, 'The Golden Stool that was born on a Friday', and has precedence over its occupant, the Asantehene. It has its own throne, the *Hwɛdɔmtea*, and its own set of regalia, including state umbrellas, a shield made of elephant skin and a gold-plated drum and lute. It also has its own bodyguard and other attendants.

An alleged request by a former British Governor of the country, Sir Frederic Hodgson, for the stool to be brought out for him to sit on, was the immediate cause of the last of the armed conflicts between the British and the Ashanti, the 1900 Rising.

Ceremonial stools are used as seats by chiefs when they sit in state or are performing rites connected with the ancestral cult. They also feature prominently at their installation when the chiefs are placed on them three consecutive times as a sign of their enthronement or enstoolment. In states which have only one or two black stools, the ceremonial stool is handed down from one ruler to another; while in states where there is a black stool to each deceased ruler, the ceremonial stool is made by the reigning monarch. When he dies it is in turn blackened and preserved in his memory as a black stool. The ceremonial stool of a chief who was deposed before his death is not blackened, but it may be retained as an extra ceremonial stool for his successors.

The point of interest in a ceremonial stool, which later may become a black stool, is how it is shaped and ornamented, for the shape and ornament may have their symbolic meanings. Originally the stool was a more or less shapeless object cut from the solid wood with only a simple handle to help

Top A *hwedɔm* chair of the Wenchi-hene, Brong-Ahafo, with foot-rest before it. The chair is decorated with brass round-headed nails, *ankaahono*, and the back is crowned with *ntuatire* modelled after a sliced calabash. The legs are of the *nkyinkyim* or spiral design. The foot-rest, *krokowa*, is covered with red felt and decorated with talismans and a horn also made of felt.

Foot An imposing *nnamu* or *akon-kromfi* armchair of the Berekumhene, Brong-Ahafo, with an exquisitely de-signed back. The design on the top bar of the back has in the centre the leaf of a kola tree, *besehene*, and on either side of it the leaves of another tree, *konin*, which has a striking resemblance to the kola tree. The design is meant to depict a saying about these two kinds of leaf, namely, that it requires a wise man to distinguish between them – '*Konin ne Besehene yɛfa no Banyansafo*'. The design in the centre of the back and on the lower bar are varieties of stylized ram's horns, *dwennimmɛn notasoɔ*. The arm-rests, of coil design, are completely plated with silver and the chair is further adorned with *ankaahono* nails and the back crowned with silver *ntuatire* eagle's claws. In front of the chair lies its foot-rest covered with red felt with decorations of talismans and horns pinned to it and held in place by a rod wrapped in a lion skin. The chair is said to have been made by the founder of the state, Nana Amankwa Diawuo, some two hundred and eighty years ago.

22

Top An elegant *nnamu* or *akonkromfi* armchair of the Wenchihene, Brong-Ahafo. The black colour of the chair gives a special lustre to its profuse silver repoussé decoration. The back of the chair has a circular *kontonkurowi* and it is flanked on either side by a decoration of triangles called *adwensa*. The *kontonkurowi* encircles a four-pointed star enclosing a boss, which is regarded as God's special star, *Nyanko Nsoromma*. It is said of this star that its special brilliance is not of its own making but is derived from its maker, God. The coil design of the arm-rest is called *apompon*. It represents a meandering path or stream of which it is said that no matter how much it meanders, it must end somewhere. In front of the chair are two foot-rests representing elephants covered in leopard skin.

Foot A fine *akonkromfi* armchair of the Agogohene, Ashanti-Akim. The central design of the back is a *kontonkurowi* with flourishes. The remaining designs are based on *dwennimmɛn* or ram's horns.

in moving it about. It was then known as a *dufua* or log. In its later development it was given three parts, namely, the top or seat, the base, and the legs or supporting column coming between the seat and the base. The black stool of Wenchi has the appearance of a *dufua*.

The stool, with all these parts, is carved out of one piece of wood. The carving begins with a prayer or libation to the spirit of the tree out of which the wood is obtained, usually *sɛsɛ* (*Funtumia africana*) or *nyame dua* (*Alstonia boonei*), and to the tools to be used, simple adzes, knives, chisels and awls.

It is the design of the column, *sɛkyɛdua*, which gives the stool its name and special character. It may be the craftsman's representation of a human being, an animal, a vegetable, any object or phenomenon of his fancy, a court scene, an incident in the history of his state or chiefdom, a proverb or maxim, or a special message which the chief for whom the stool is made wishes to give to his people.

Kontonkurowi, a circular design, is fairly commonly used to represent the orbit of the moon. This is to symbolize the saying, '*Kontonkurowi, ɛda amansan nyinaa kɔn mu*', meaning that there is no part of the earth nor any nation that does not behold the orbit of the moon when it shines. This may be taken to represent the power of a fighting ruler which is sure to be felt by all his enemies.

The column of the present Asantehene's personal ceremonial stool embodies a carved knot, called the knot of wisdom, *nyansa pɔ* (a reef knot), to symbolize the promise he gave to his people on his accession to the Golden Stool that he would bind the nation together by prudent administration.

Rulers who are so entitled by tradition may decorate the seat, column and base of their ceremonial stools with designs (*adwinneɛ*) in silver or gold or both. The designs vary and, as with the column design, a stool may be named according to the decorative design used. This is usually one, or a combination of any, of the following: horizontal or vertical bars or bands; crosses (the Greek cross and St Andrew's cross are the most common); moon and stars; crescents; circular or rosette patterns embodying floral designs; or stylized animal forms such as that of a crocodile. The silver decoration on the seat of the Berekumhene's ceremonial stool, for example, includes stars and crescents, which illustrate a saying that the moon may die but not the stars.

A ceremonial stool usually has attached to it a bell or a number of bells of cast-iron or brass. Thus it is sometimes referred to as *adɔnnwa*, the bell

Top The Golden Stool of Ashanti. Believed to have descended from the skies in the seventeenth century through the incantations of Kɔmfo Anɔkye, Chief Priest of the King of Ashanti, Nana Osei Tutu. It was presented to the people as enshrining the soul of the nation and symbolizing their unity and the authority of their ruler. It has been regarded as a sacred object, the gift of the gods, and has been a source of inspiration to chivalrous deeds.

It is a mass of solid gold. It stands about a foot and a half from the ground and the seat is about two feet long and one foot wide. Among the objects strapped to it are cast gold effigies of defeated warriors used as bells, one gold and two brass cast bells, and precious beads, *suman*. As the Golden Stool must never be allowed to touch the ground, it is placed on its special throne, the *Hwɛdɔmtea*, which in turn rests on an elephant skin, *banwoma*.

Foot A *nnamu* or *akonkromfi* armchair of the Dormaahene, Ruler of the Dormaa State, Brong-Ahafo, with a back of perforated designs, arm-rests with coil designs and gently sloping legs supported by elaborately shaped struts. Parts of the body of the chair are ornamented with gold leaf. In front of the chair lies a *puduo* or *kokruwa*, a foot-rest of red and black felt cloth, *nkrawoɔkɔkɔɔ* and *nkrawoɔbiri*; the foot-rest is decorated with a gold boss of stylized ram's horns and two pads, one on either side of the boss, each bearing five cowries. The *puduo* contains a charm which gives protection to the Dormaahene. The chair rests on a lion skin and the foot-rest on a leopard skin. They were both made by the Dormaahene Nana Oppong Yaw about 1860.

stool. The number of bells indicates the status of the chief to whom the stool belongs.

CHAIRS

Another kind of ceremonial seat is the *asipim* chair. Its original form was the *akɛntɛnnwa* or *apɛntɛnnwa*, a cane chair. The framework was of wood and the seat of cane woven into chequers. The earliest type of *asipim* chair is still used, but nowadays mostly by ordinary citizens.

In time the cane material used for the seat, *demire* (a rattan palm), was replaced by antelope hide, of the kind used for the membrane of a drum and the scabbard of ceremonial swords. Brass nails were used instead of the original strings of cane to fasten together the parts of the chair and to hold the hide for the seat taut.

With these new materials, the *akɛntɛnnwa* became a much stronger chair and it was therefore renamed *asipim*, which may be translated as 'I stand firm'.

The brass nails were of two kinds, the *mpeaboɔ* and the *ankaahono*. The *mpeaboɔ* was so called because it was shaped like the gold-weight used for weighing gold-dust levied as war tax, and the *ankaahono* because it resembled a sliced orange. The *mpeaboɔ* was more often used for the *asipim*; if the *ankaahono* was used, the chair was referred to not as *asipim* but also as *ankaahono*.

Further developments led to changes in the size, height and general appearance of the chair. Smaller, round-headed nails in bands of several lines, and elaborate repoussé metalwork, were used to adorn the main body of the chair. These were mostly in brass, but silver was also used by those entitled to do so. In some cases the back of the chair had embossed circular patterns, like those found on the seat of ornamented stools, and triangles, sometimes enhanced by hachures or hatching.

The *asipim* could be given a low seat and a sturdy square shape, in which case it would be called *asipimtia* or low *asipim*, convenient for chiefs of below average height. The other type, *asipimtenten*, had a high seat and oblong shape.

Underneath the seat of any *asipim* chair usually hung a talisman charm (*suman*) to give protection to the chief while seated.

Later developments of the *asipim* chair were the *hwɛdɔm* and the *nnamu* or *akonkromfi* chairs – in that order. These had more elaborate design and

Top A simple but beautifully designed chair with the back and arm-rests draped in cloth patterned like leopard skin. It is affixed to two poles and used as a palanquin borne on the shoulders of four men.

Foot A set of cushions, one placed on a coarse cloth blanket, *nsaa*, spread on the ground, and three others propped against a model of a branch of a *Nyame Dua* or Tree of God. *Nyame Dua* or its branch is used by the Akan as an altar to the Supreme Deity. The branch has three prongs at the top on which is placed a basin or pot for offerings to the Supreme Deity. It is covered with fine leather and ornamented with gold rings and talismans. The cushion on the ground, *pintaa*, is covered with silk and velvet. The set of cushions is used by the Asantehene when in mourning or grief as a throne instead of his ornate stools and chairs. (See p. 15.)

ornamentation. Some of them were given arm-rests, of plain or coil design, and curved legs joined by struts or bars of plait or other designs.

The back of the *hwɛdɔm* was usually plain, sometimes decorated with embossed circular patterns; but the *akonkromfi* had a back of exquisite perforated patterns. The back of both the *hwɛdɔm* and the *akonkromfi* was also surmounted with knobs (*ntuatire*) of various designs such as a calabash, a grease-pot or an abstract of an eagle's claws.

Hwɛdɔm literally means 'facing the fold or the enemy'. It was used by the ruler when he sat in state to declare war against an enemy country. In peacetime it was principally used when the chief presided over a court session or a business meeting with his councillors. The *akonkromfi* was so called because it was thought to resemble the pose of a praying mantis. It was also called *nnamu* because sitting in it gave one a restful posture. This was used on joyous ceremonial occasions.

It has been contended that the designs of the *hwɛdɔm* and the *akonkromfi* look foreign and may be copies of European designs introduced by early Portuguese and Dutch traders. If this view is established, however, it makes nonsense of the history given to me of the evolution of the *asipim* chair.

CHAPTER TWO

Swords and Other Weapons

The next most important of the chief's regalia, after stools, skins and chairs, are weapons of all descriptions. These originated as implements for domestic, hunting, farming and military purposes; but in time some of them assumed certain social and ritual functions. Principal among these weapons are spears, arrows, clubs, swords and guns. These will be examined separately and mention will be made of their accessories such as the baldric of swords and the bandolier of guns. It must be observed that, as items of regalia, spears, arrows and clubs predominate in the open country of the north, while swords and guns are chiefly used in the forest areas of the south.

SPEARS

The spear may be a weapon of solid steel, with a leaf-shaped piercing point or head. The other end may be broad and unsharpened or may have another piercing point like the head.

On the other hand, the spear may be composite, made in parts, consisting of the steel or brass head, leaf-shaped or bifurcated; the foreshaft, linking the head and the main shaft; and the shaft itself. The foreshaft may be of brass and the shaft of wood ornamented with strips of leather, coloured felt or leopard skin, as, for example, some of the spears of the Nayiri, head of the Mamprusi State, and the Ya Na, head of the Dagombas; in either case the spears are called *kpana*. The spearhead, like the head of an arrow, is bathed in poison to make its thrust deadly. The custodian of the *kpana* is called the *kpanadana* and he uses the spear or spears to protect his ruler.

The Nayiri has other spears in his own possession which he will use if the *kpanadana* fails him. Spears are now mostly used for ceremonial purposes, being held before the ruler when he appears in state or is receiving outside dignitaries.

The spear is now hardly found among the regalia of any of the rulers of Southern Ghana, although, as a military weapon, it must have been used by the southern peoples at an early stage in their history. The Akans call the levy raised for preparing for a battle *apeatɔ*, or 'spear toll', the Akan word for spear being *pea*.

BOWS AND ARROWS

Arrows, called *china* (the initial 'c' is hard) by the Kasenas of the north, are made of small bamboo sticks and have poisonous steel piercing heads. They are carried about in a quiver, also made of bamboo and usually covered all over with the hide of a goat, sheep, cow or crocodile; they have embroidered and incised designs, relieved in places with coloured felt. The quiver is borne over the left shoulder suspended from a similarly ornamented leather strap.

The arrows are shot from a bow with a string made from the skin of a duiker and a wooden stave; the latter is sometimes ornamented, like the quiver, with felt and leather. A bracer, made of ornamented leather and containing a charm, is worn on the left wrist of the archer to strengthen it when releasing the arrows.

The southern peoples must also have used arrows and other missiles at one stage or other in their history but the only survivor is the catapult still used by children. Certainly the Akwamu armies had bowmen as late as the eighteenth century.

The Akan word for arrows is *agyan*, pronounced as '*ahjan*'.

CLUBS

A club as a weapon is designed to strike a crushing blow. Clubs used by chiefs in Northern Ghana, such as the *jamgbee* of the Yendis and the *damire* of the Mamprusis, are credited with magical powers, so that they are not only capable of causing physical harm but also of driving away evil spirits. Thus the club has become one of the most important items of regalia in Northern Ghana, and it is one which every ruler must possess. Wives of rulers, at least the senior ones, also have their official clubs. When a chief dies, the club which he used in life is preserved in his memory, fulfilling the same function as the black stool in Southern Ghana.

The prestige and ritual value of the club now obscure its original use as a weapon, and this development is confirmed by the look of the club. Instead of a crude cudgel, one finds a slender stick wrapped with leather, felt, brass or silver, or a combination of any of these. It may have a knob

Top A young sword-bearer carrying his sword with an *abɔsodeɛ* of a fish and wearing a cap of eagle's feathers, *ntakrakyɛ*. The cap is adorned with a gold boss of ram's horns.

Foot Nana Kwabena Owusa, Edwesohene, Ashanti, dressed in his *batakarikɛseɛ*, a smock decorated with ornamental talismans, with its corresponding hat and neck-wear, with a *sɛpɔ* knife in his mouth and holding a gun. This costume is used when going to war or holding a state funeral.

31

Top The *Flasi* of the Ruler of the Mafi State of Tongu, Volta Region. He fulfils more or less the same role as the *Ɔkra* of an Akan ruler. He also acts as a kind of mascot for the army of his state. He is dressed in a smock dyed brown and a cap of the same material, both adorned with a number of charms including cowries, talismans, an eagle's claws and the tail of a brush-tailed porcupine. The white clay on his face is believed to have the effect of diverting gun-shots and the bundle of vulture feathers which he holds keeps death from the army on the battlefield.

Foot One of the *abrofoɔ*, constabulary, of the Ruler of the Kwahu State, Eastern Region, reciting the history of the state and the heroic deeds of past rulers by pointing his sword towards the Ruler. He wears his leopard-skin cap of office, *krɔbɔnkyɛ*. The recitations are made when the Ruler sits or proceeds in state. While in the procession he is obliged by custom to stop and listen, no matter how tired he may be; he is also expected not to smile during the recitation; if he does, he must pacify the narrator.

of some shape at the head, a wrist-loop at the grip and a spike at the end of the shaft touching the ground, but it is hardly recognizable as a club and may perhaps be more properly referred to as a mace or rod of office.

The close resemblance between these ornate clubs of the north and the staves or sticks of office of 'linguists' or spokesmen of chiefs in the south would suggest that the latter originated from the clubs carried by the chiefs.

In this connection, it is relevant to observe that the Nayiri has two of these rods which are in the custody of one of his palace officials, the *naaso*; when he himself is not holding one of them, the *naaso* holds one, sitting in front of him as linguists in the south do with their staves. It is also a tradition that linguist-sticks (which will be discussed later) and other protective weapons, such as swords, are kept with the black stools in the stool-houses of the south. It could be inferred that the stick, regarded as a club, and the other weapons are meant to protect the stool.

SWORDS

Swords are of various designs and used for several purposes. For example, among the regalia of the Asantehene no fewer than six different kinds of state swords can be distinguished according to their use. Broadly speaking, a sword has the following three parts.

Blade: This is usually of steel; but one of the principal swords of the Fiaga, chief of Ho in the Volta Region, is made of solid ivory. The blade may be designed for cutting or piercing or both and it usually has incised lines or symbolic designs on it. For example, towards the piercing point of the ivory sword of the Fiaga of Ho is a drawing of a chameleon, symbolizing what is said of the ruler, that he never hurries but all the same achieves his ends. Certain swords have two or three blades which converge at the top where they fit into the hilt, *mfenasa*.

Hilt: This is made up of the grip and the pommel which prevents the hilt from slipping through the hand. This is further crowned by another knob or cone. The hilt is usually made of wood, such as *ɔfemma* (*Microdesmis puberula*), and wrapped with gold leaf on which are worked irregular and wavy lines, dots, chevrons, zigzags and other geometrical patterns. The *banchiriga* sword of the Ya Na of Northern Ghana has a bone hilt. One of the swords of the Denkyirahene of the Western Region, which is only carried by twins, has a triple hilt, *mfenasa*.

33

Swords and Other Weapons

Most of the various types of sword are carried over the left shoulder and their shape is as has been described. But the *afenatene*, literally the long sword, is differently shaped and is not carried about but planted in the ground. It has a triple blade, much shorter than that of the other swords in proportion to the rest of the sword, and between it and the hilt is a long shaft of various decorative forms such as plaits and spirals. Instead of the ordinary knob or cone which crowns the pommel of the other types of sword, the *afenatene* is topped by a symbolic model, for example, of an eagle carrying away a bone and being watched by a dog in disgust. The model may be in wood but is plated with gold.

Sheath: The blades of some swords are encased in sheaths or scabbards made – rarely – of brass, or – more usually – of the skins of various animals such as goats or leopards. Sometimes hanging from the sheath is a gold cast of some fruit, animal or human being, illustrating some maxim, a message from the ruler who uses it or an incident in the history of the chiefdom. This is called the *abɔsodeɛ*. One example is of a tsetse fly resting on the back of a tortoise; it is said of it that it can do no harm since it cannot suck the tortoise's blood. Perhaps the *abɔsodeɛ* is the equivalent of the gilt model found on top of the pommel of the *afenatene*.

Also affixed to either side of the scabbard is a round gold boss between the top of the scabbard and the bottom of the hilt. It is called *nnɛm* and is probably only for purposes of decoration. It gives a solid ending to the scabbard and its roundness reflects the spherical shape of the hilt.

The type of sword described above is used mostly in Southern Ghana and for ceremonial purposes, not for cutting or piercing. Swords, such as the *takobi* of the Nayiri, Head of the Mamprusi State, are also used in the north; but these, like other weapons found in chiefs' regalia there, for example, knives, hatchets and axes, are actually used as offensive or defensive weapons and not for ceremonial purposes.

Ceremonial Swords: The following distinctions are made between ceremonial swords according to their use. There are also corresponding slight structural distinctions. In most states there is a distinction between *akrafena*, used in the ritual for purifying the soul of the ruler and the black stool of state, and the *akofena*, also called the *nsuaefena*. The latter is called *akofena* because it is a survivor of the swords used in the past in war, usually the actual sword of the founder of the state. It is also called *nsuaefena* because it is the sword which the ruler uses when taking the oath of office at his installation; it is also used by his elders when swearing the oath of

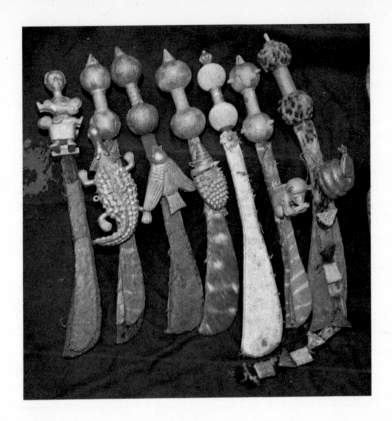

Top Ceremonial swords of the Ruler of the Kwahu State, Eastern Region, showing *abɔsodeɛ* or gold casts, of the following (*left to right*): a mother of twins, a crocodile, a butterfly, a turtle, a monkey helping itself to a grasshopper, and a Gaboon viper to which is attached a belt decorated with gold and silver talismans. The white sword, an *akrafena* or sword of the soul, has no *abɔsodeɛ* but has a gold circular boss, *nnɛm*, at the top of the sheath.

Foot Spears of the Nayiri, Ruler of the Mamprusi State, Northern Ghana. The staffs are decorated with leopard skin and felt.

allegiance to him. It is further used as a badge of credence by those who go on the ruler's errands.

The scabbard and the hilt of the *akrafena* are painted white with a clay substance, *hyire*. The grip and the cone on the pommel of the hilt are sometimes decorated with gold leaf, and a gold boss separates the sheath from the hilt. An *abɔsodeɛ* may also be placed on the scabbard.

More distinctions are to be seen between the swords of rulers of older and richer dynasties such as those of Akim Abuakwa, Akim Kotoku, Akwamu, Denkyira, Dormaa and Takyiman. As already mentioned, the Asantehene has at least six categories of swords used for different purposes, namely:

Kɛtɛanofena	Made up of *akrafena* and *bosomfena*, serving more or less the same purposes as the *akrafena* and *nsuaefena* already mentioned.
Dɔmfonsan	Used on the battlefield for swearing the oath of fidelity and for leading the army. It forms part of the normal accoutrement of a soldier. This is the original form of state sword.
Afenatene	Used as a complement to or substitute for *kɛtɛanofena*.
Asomfofena	Accompanying the Golden Stool and used by couriers sent to distant lands, for example, to announce a death in the royal lineage, or sent with a herald to declare war against an enemy.
Abrafoɔfena	Looking more like a bayonet than a sword and used by the constabulary, *abrafoɔ*.
Sɛpɔ	Small knives used in the past by executioners for thrusting through the cheeks of their victims to prevent them uttering a curse.
Ahoprafoɔfena	Used by the king's followers who carry elephant-, horse- or cow-tail fly-whisks.

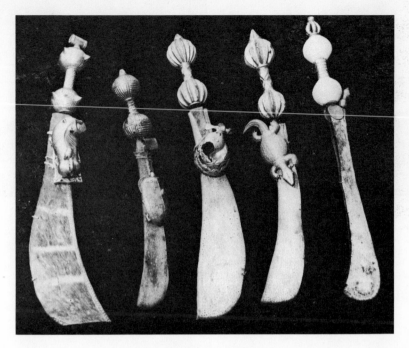

Ceremonial swords of the Berekumhene, Brong-Ahafo, with gilded hilts and the following *abɔsodeɛ* on the scabbards (*left* to *right*):

(a) A lion on the sheath and a keg of gunpowder surmounting the hilt, illustrating the saying that no one challenges a lion unarmed.

(b) A tortoise with a fly standing on its back, symbolizing the proverb which says that a fly stands on the back of a tortoise in vain as its sting cannot pierce the tortoise's shell.

(c) A Gaboon viper holding a bird it has caught in its mouth. It is said the viper never attacks without provocation.

(d) A monitor lizard, regarded as the symbol of a peacemaker. It is said a peacemaker does no one any harm.

(e) An *akrafena*, sword of the *kra* or soul without an *abɔsodeɛ*. Crowning the hilt is a *foa*, an ornament also used as an umbrella top. It is said to be an imitation of the Bawku stool of Northern Ghana. The miniature sword seen projecting from the sheath illustrates the saying '*Afena bi da ebi so*'. (Some swords are more powerful than others.)

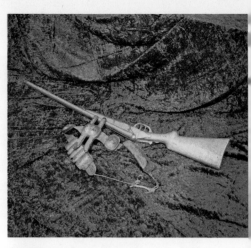

Kit, *ntoa*, of the bodyguard of the Ruler of the Effutu State (Winneba), Atuntumfoɔ, Central Region, two of leopard skin and the third of elephant skin, with their corresponding shoulder-belts, and a skullcap decorated with gold shells. Attached to the haversacks are small *sɛpɔ* knives with gilt handles encased in leather sheaths decorated with gold leaf.

Gilded gun with shoulder-belt of the Techimanhene's bodyguard, Brong-Ahafo.

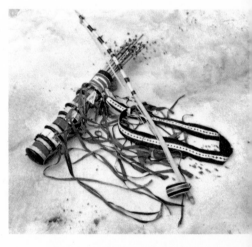

The pots and pans, clothes and other personal belongings of the senior wife of the Ya Na, Northern Ghana, bound together in a net and placed in an enamel basin. The complete unit is called *kpanjogu* and is assembled when the senior wife is travelling or joining her husband in the palace for the first time after the marriage.

Arrows in a quiver of bamboo wrapped in leather and coloured felt with a strap attached, and a partially decorated bow with an ornate bracer at one end. They belong to the Navropio, Northern Ghana.

Swords and Other Weapons

A mysterious sword called *Afena Kwaw*, of the Adansi State in Ashanti, is believed to have descended from heaven at the time of the foundation of the state, and is held to be the symbol of the state's unity and of the authority of its head.

Sword-bearers form an important group of the chief's entourage since, apart from their other duties, they are responsible for the purification rites for the souls of the chief and his predecessors. In certain states, such as Akwamu and Akim Abuakwa, a child of this group is chosen to represent the souls, and he is called the *Ɔkra*, 'The Soul'.

Special kit is provided for these sword-bearers, which consists of a skull-cap made of the feathers of a bird or the skin of an animal, a baldric for the sword when not in use, an item of neckwear consisting of white cord supporting a pendant breastplate (*ayaneɛ*), a bag for snuff, herbs, rations etc. (*amiadeɛ*), and sometimes another piece of neckwear consisting of an iron chain (*atweaban*).

GUNS

Guns as military weapons have been in use in Ghana for centuries. At one time the Portuguese traded in firearms at Elmina, and other firearms were introduced at various times by the other European nations trading in Africa. Efforts were made to manufacture guns locally, but with little success, owing to the difficulty of obtaining iron ore; they resulted in the *humu* gun, made of brass, so called because of the barrel which was absurdly large.

Guns have also come to be used for hunting, and it has become customary for guns to be fired at the funerals of chiefs and distinguished citizens and at some traditional dances, such as the *Asafo*. This use of the gun at dances and at funerals may, however, only point to the military power of the people.

The bodyguard of a chief on ceremonial occasions guard him with ceremonial guns. Those of the Asantehene and other senior rulers are richly adorned with gold or silver decorations on the butt, the barrel and the end of the barrel. The ceremonial kit of the bodyguard comprises a skullcap made of the skin of some animal – elephant, goat or leopard; a pouch or haversack for provisions with one or two straps for holding *sɛpɔ* knives; a bandolier or shoulder belt, also with several straps for holding *sɛpɔ* knives; and a horn or container (*danka*) for gunpowder or bullets. The whole kit is called *ntoa*.

Afenatene swords of the Ruler of the Akim Abuakwa State, Eastern Region.

A haversack and bandolier made of leopard skin, being part of the equipment, *ntoa*, of the bodyguard of the Kumawuhene, Ashanti. Gold-plated *sɛpɔ* knives and golden shells are affixed to both of them. Hanging from the bandolier are two small bells seen on either side of the haversack. Below the haversack is a sword decorated on the sheath with golden shells. This is an *ahoprafoɔ* sword, borne by fly-whisk bearers.

A *bosomru akrafena* sword of the Techimanhene, Brong-Ahafo, and the cap of its bearer. It is the principal sword of the state and is used in the purification rites for the Ruler's soul. The leather scabbard and the pommel are painted white with a vegetable oil. The knob crowning the pommel is a gold cast of a fruit called *bɔbɔmfrada*, and the gold circular boss separating the scabbard from the hilt has a design based on the leaves of groundnuts and so called *nkatehoon*. The grasp of the hilt is embossed with gold leaf and underneath the boss, *nnɛm*, is a replica of the sword with a gilded hilt.

The cap, made of duiker hide, is decorated on the top with the cast of a bird carrying a cannon and cannon-balls on its wings. It also carries a keg of gunpowder in its beak, and on the sides of the hat are more cannon-balls. The bird, *adwetakyi*, proverbially is said to be so powerful that it requires a cannon to shoot it dead: '*Adwetakyi anoma wrenfoɔ, ono na yede apremo ne aboɔ sane no.*'

Women in a procession at a state durbar. Those holding guns form part of the Ruler's bodyguard.

Nkotokwaa, a pair of large leather wallets with embroidered designs, tassels and a handle decorated with leopard skin. They are containers for gold dust and the apparatus used for weighing it. Like the *apemadaka*, treasury boxes, *nkotokwaa* are always used in pairs. They belong to the Kumawuhene, Ashanti.

CHAPTER THREE

The Treasury

The peoples of Ghana have had various forms of currency in the course of their history, apart from the barter system. The original currency was iron (*dutu*), followed successively by brass (*yaawa*), cowries (*sedeɛ*), gold dust (*sika futuro*) and silver (*dwetɛ*).

When gold dust came to be used, because of the precious nature of the metal, care was taken that only the proper quantity was parted with, and this led to a system of weighing and the use of what have come to be known as the Ashanti gold-weights. These had to be readily accessible to the trader or the market woman at any moment and so containers were improvised not only for the gold dust itself, together with the weights, but for all the accessories used in weighing so that these could easily be carried about. They were first wrapped up in a cloth before being put in the container.

The container used by an ordinary citizen was the *fotoɔ*; but a chief also had the *sannaa, kuduo, apemadaka* and *nkotokwaa*. It must be mentioned that not every chief in Ghana possessed all these. The use of gold dust as currency was limited to Southern Ghana, particularly to the Akans. The *sannaa, kuduo* and *nkotokwaa* may have been used by a fair number of the principal Akan rulers; but it was certainly not so in the case of the *apemadaka*.

The *fotoɔ* and *sannaa* are broad folded pieces of the skin of certain animals. The *fotoɔ* is made from that of an African civet cat (*kankane*) or of a Diana monkey (*boapeaa*), the *sannaa* from the ear of an elephant. The *fotoɔ* contained weights none of which exceeded a *piredwan* (£8) in value; these were the weights used in ordinary trading. The *sannaa* contained weights of the same denomination as those found in the *fotoɔ*, but also larger ones, some of values exceeding *mpiredwan du* (£80). The larger weights were used to measure gold dust required for state functions such as the *Adɛɛ* festivals or royal funerals, or for a ransom fee, that is, a payment in lieu of a death penalty (*atitɔdeɛ*), or an indemnity fee required of a defeated chiefdom.

Sometimes the whole *fotoɔ* was placed in another bag, particularly when

43

it was being taken on a long journey; such a bag was the *nkotokwaa*, made of fine leather with embroidered decorations. There was usually a pair of these bags with straps to hang over the shoulder. One of the Asantehene's pairs of *nkotokwaa* has a golden padlock, the other a silver padlock.

Gold dust, without weights and the accessories for weighing, was also kept in a *kuduo*. The *kuduo*, a beautifully shaped and engraved brass vessel or bowl, is considered to be one of the finest types of West African metal-work. Some have lids; others are designed without them. The *kuduo* was also used as a ceremonial vessel to contain offerings for certain religious and civic rites, and instances have been known of the *kuduo* being reverenced as a shrine. Trinkets, *bɔdɔm* or *aggrey* beads, and other valuables were also kept in a *kuduo*.

The *apemadaka*, like the *nkotokwaa*, were used in pairs. They are wooden boxes which are sometimes draped in beautiful felt cloths. One cloth is of a gold colour, the other green. Each contained gold dust worth £1,000 (*suruboɔ apem*), hence the name *apemadaka*.

Gold-weights (*abrammoɔ*) are perhaps the best known of Ghana's artefacts; they and wooden fertility dolls are usually used to represent Ghana in books on African art. They are made of copper, bronze or brass by the *cire-perdue* method of casting, from wax models enclosed in clay. The wax is melted and allowed to run out and the molten metal is poured into the clay mould that is left.

The weights normally weigh from 0.02 grammes upwards; the heaviest known is 1,385 grammes. The ordinary ones for trading purposes measure not more than an inch or two in length, breadth or diameter. The value of single weights in sterling ranges from ½d. (*poa huu*) to £80 (*mpiredwan du*). These weights are still used by certain rulers, for example when gold dust is required for the burial of someone connected with the ruler; but today the real interest in the weights for a student of Ghanaian society lies in their design and in their symbolic meanings.

The weights can be divided into four broad categories as far as subject-matter is concerned: those portraying human forms and the fauna of the country; those representing the country's flora; those representing inanimate objects of every description, such as the items of a chief's regalia; and those of geometrical or purely ornamental design. Weights of the first three categories are sometimes allegorical in that they symbolize certain maxims or proverbs or the people's notions about life generally, or depict the scene of some rite or ceremony. Those representing regalia are

Top A *kuduo* or casket in bronze, used as a container for gold dust, trinkets, precious beads and other valuables as well as for offerings in connection with certain religious and civil rites. The fine craftsmanship of this *kuduo* is unparalleled. On the lid are figurines like those of gold-weights, representing a chief smoking a pipe and being entertained to music by royal musicians. Believed to have been made for Nana Kofi Karikari, Asantehene, it was taken during one of the Anglo-Ashanti wars but returned to the present Asantehene who in turn has donated it to the Prempeh II Jubliee Museum, Kumasi. The body of the *kuduo* itself and its intricately shaped hasp are magnificently engraved.

Foot Two *apemadaka* or treasury boxes of the Akwamuhene, Eastern Region. Gold dust to the value of £1,000, *suruboɔ apem*, was in the past kept in each of these boxes, hence the name *apemadaka* (the box worth £1,000). One is decorated with brass nails, *mprɛngo*, and the other has brass repoussé decoration.

45

purposely made to serve as models from which copies can be made of lost regalia or those abandoned on the battlefield.

A figurative weight may portray a single person, animal or object, or it may be a composite piece showing a number of persons, animals or objects. A ladder by itself, for example, will be illustrative of the saying that the ladder of death is not meant for one person only; everyone will have to climb it some day. In other words, death is no respecter of persons – *owuo atwedeɛ baako mfo*. An example of a composite figurative weight is a bird caught in a trap, symbolizing the saying that a wise bird is caught with a simple trap or that he who prides himself on being cunning sometimes unwittingly betrays his weaknesses – *anomaa nitefoɔ, fidie yi no ntɛntɛnoa*. An instance of a weight depicting a scene is that of a chief sacrificing a fowl to his ancestors, which is a reflection on the sacrificial aspect of the ancestor cult in Akan religion. The sacrifice of a fowl is an exception to the normal practice which is the sacrifice of a sheep. For interest, further examples of figurative weights are given at the end of this chapter. They are unclassified.

Weights of geometrical or ornamental design are considered the first to have been used. The designs consist of straight or wavy lines, chevrons, zigzags, triangles, dots, circles, spirals, coils, crosses, swastikas and similar patterns. They are said to be symbolic, as in the case of the other types of weight, although with most of them it is difficult, if not impossible, to decipher what they symbolize. Some of them, however, are known to represent certain objects, for example, the horns of a ram, the flow of a stream or a particular *coiffure*. The designs are identical with some of the patterns found on the *adinkra* stamped cloths which are regarded as amulet signs or Moslem symbols.

The accessories used for the weighing of gold dust are scales (*nsania*), spoons (*saawa*) for lifting it and placing it on the scales, shovels (*famfa*) for scooping it up to remove dust and other foreign matter, and boxes (*abampruwa*) for storing it in. All these are made of brass. The spoons and boxes have beautiful engraved designs; sometimes miniatures of them are included among the weights. It is said that the Takyimanhene in the Brong-Ahafo Region once had weights and accessories of gold.

Top The keys of Christiansborg Castle, Accra, which the Akwamus of the Eastern Region seized from the Danish traders in June 1693. The keys were retained when the Akwamus resold the Castle to the Danes in the following year. They have sinced formed part of the Akwamuhene's treasury.

Foot The *sannaa* or treasury bag of Kɔmfo Anɔkye (late seventeenth century) in which it is said he deposited presents made to him by the chiefs and people of Ashanti after he had called down the Golden Stool from the skies. The precise contents are not known. As a *sannaa*, however, the contents will include gold dust and apparatus for its weighing.

The bag is at the Prempeh II Jubilee Museum, Kumasi, on loan from the Ruler of Agona, Ashanti, descendant of Kɔmfo Anɔkye and the present occupant of his stool.

Anɔkye ordered that the bag should never be opened for fear of its precious contents going astray, and indeed it has never been opened since his time. The bag is made of elephant skin and rests on an exquisitely designed brass basin.

Examples of Figurative Weights

A crocodile swallowing a mudfish	*Pitire kɛseɛ a ɔda bunu mu ɔmemene adeɛ a ɔmemene ma ne wura dɛnkyɛm.*
	If the mudfish in the stream grows fat, it does so to the advantage of the crocodile (to whom it may fall a victim at any time). *The prosperity of a servant is to the advantage of his master.*

Two crocodiles with a common stomach (Siamese crocodiles!)	*Funtumfunafu ne dɛnkyɛmfunafu; yɛn afuru ko, nso yɛdidi a na yɛrefom.*
	Two crocodiles who have a common stomach and yet fight over food they both come across. *This symbol makes fun of greediness and egoism. The food goes into the same stomach, no matter which of them takes it. The crocodiles are alleged to rebut this by saying that the enjoyment of food involves not only the stomach but the palate as well.*

A hunchback	*Afu si wǎnim a wogye, ɛsi wǎkyi a wogye.* There is hardly anything one can do about a hump, whether it develops on one's chest or back. *Do not kick against the inevitable.*

An elephant-tail whisk	*Ɛsono dua-ɛyɛ tia, ɔde saa ara na ɛpra ne ho.* The elephant is capable of whisking off flies with his tail, short as it is. *Unavoidable handicaps should not be used as an excuse for inactivity or laziness.*

A farmer smoking a pipe	*Okuafoɔ yɛ adwuma a Ɔgye nǎhome.* Even the farmer has time for relaxation. *'All work and no play makes Jack a dull boy.'*
	Another version of this symbol is someone carrying a keg of gunpowder and yet smoking a pipe, illustrating the saying that carrying gunpowder is no reason for not smoking – yɛso atuduro a yɛnom taa.

A herbalist scraping the bark of a tree	*Ɔbaako wɛrɛ aduro a, ɛgu.* The bark of a tree falls to the ground if the one scraping it has no one else to collect it for him. *It is unwise to refuse help which one needs.*
An okro fruit	*Nkrumakɛsɛ, ɔbɔ ne yaa hyɛ ne yam.* The okro does not reveal its seeds through its skin. *Suffer in silence. There is more in a man's mind than shows in his face.*
A bunch of plantains	*Wogu apem gu abrane a gye sɛ wode ba kuro kɛseɛ mu.* The farmer must send his crops to the town if he wishes to find a good market for them. *Good and useful work can be acknowledged only by those who see its value.*
A hedgehog	*Apɛsɛ yɛ kɛseɛ a ɔyɛ ma dufɔkyeɛ.* It is the rotten wood, or the worms in it, that help the hedgehog to grow fat; hence the hedgehog is often found hiding under rotten wood. *One cannot escape some obligation to one's benefactors.*
Birds in a nest	*Anomaa nua ne deɛ ɔne no da pirebuo mu.* A bird's relation is the one with which it shares a common nest. *'Birds of a feather flock together' – common problems bring together those who are affected by them.*
A hunter being attacked by a leopard	*Sɛ wobɛto ɔsebɔ tuo na wanwuo deɛ, fanyinam. . . .* Better not to have fired at all than to have shot at a leopard and missed killing it. *'Don't bite off more than you can chew.'*

49

A set of gold-weights with geometrical designs. The predominant swastika is believed to be a stylized form of the symbol of the two crocodiles with a common stomach. (See p. 48.)

A set of gold-weights, including versions of a pyramidal object. One of the pyramids is surmounted by a cannon. Another (*top left*) has standing on it a *toakyiraafa* bird (bird with its head thrown back), signifying the saying that one must not ignore one's past experience. Two other of the pyramids have the symbol of two birds fighting with their beaks. (See p. 53.)

Four gold-weights (*left* to *right*):
(a) A chief seated on a *kontonkurowi* stool and holding a sword and shield, the emblems of a warrior.
(b) A double gong of a herald (*ɛsɛn*), used to call attention before pronouncements.
(c) A number of birds climbing a tree with one on top, symbolizing the saying that only birds of the same species or class play together. (See p. 53.)
(d) An *akonkromfi* chair.

A miscellany of gold-weights: a pyramid with two cannons on top, a chameleon, a pod of beans, a pod of groundnuts, the pincer of a crab, a duck, birds caught in a trap, a fish, a double whip, a horn, a hoe, a fan, another fish, an axe-sword (*akuma*) and a leopard.

A scorpion	*Ana ka wo yayaya a woku no yayaya.* When the scorpion stings you mercilessly, you have to kill it in the same spirit. *A case of the 'lex talionis' – an eye for an eye and a tooth for a tooth?*
A chief on his throne	*Pånin wu a, na efie abɔ.* If the head of a household dies, that is the end of the household. *No organization can survive without sound leadership.*
A shield	*Ɛkyɛm tete a ɛka ne brɛmo.* When a shield wears out, the framework still remains. *Men die, but their words or works may live for ever.*
A water-snail	*Abebeɛ gye-sɛ wotwa ne ti ne ne to ansa na woafe no.* To suck the meat out of a water-snail, you must cut off the top and the bottom. *No good thing is gained without effort.*
Pods of kola	*Nhohoɔ tare bese ho ɔnte nwe; ɔnte ntɔn.* The red ant on the kola pod that will not pluck the kola to eat or sell. *'The dog in the manger.'*
A triangular iron design	*Yɛnkwati Firaw nkɔ Nta.* You cannot get to Northern Ghana without crossing the Volta. *The laws of nature or society must be obeyed to succeed in life.*
A climbing stem	*Ɛferɛ firi nåse na ɛbum.* The pumpkin blossoms from the roots. *A sound foundation makes for a good super-structure.*

Cartridge-belt	*Atuduro asa a ɛnyɛ Akowua ntoa mu a.* The cartridge-belt of Akowua (a celebrated warrior) has never been known to lack bullets. *A resourceful person may sometimes get into difficulties but he is never found wanting.*
A chimpanzee	*Nsoroboa di mąduane a, ɛnyɛ me ya sɛ kontromfi a ne nsa hyia sekan.* It is painful to the farmer when a chimpanzee feeds on his crops, because it is capable of handling a cutlass; it has the features of a human being and so can make a farm for itself. He does not, however, mind birds feeding on his crops. *A needless beggar is an affront to the generous.*
A guinea fowl	*Akɔmfɛm di apɔnkyerɛne funu akyiri a, ɔbɛdi ne kɔm.* If the guinea fowl goes after a dead frog, it is only going to intensify its hunger (because dead frogs are a taboo). *It is unwise to pursue a project which gives no prospects of results.*
Birds on a tree	*Nsee goro tipɛn tipɛn.* Only birds of the same species or class play together on the same tree. *Class-consciousness.*
Two fowls fighting	*Nkokɔ ntɔkwa.* Two birds fighting with their beaks. *A battle of words. No one is seriously injured by the mere exchange of angry words.*
A man with a bundle of firewood on his head	*Etire ntee a yɛnnyae adeɛ soa.* As long as the head remains, one cannot avoid carrying loads about. *A worthy cause must be pursued to the end.*

A snake on a bush path	Ɔprammire a ɔsi kwan, nåkyiri mmaa aduasa. A black-necked or spitting cobra blocking the bush path cannot avoid thirty strokes from passers-by. *Evil-doers cannot escape retribution.*
A bird, the plantain-eater	Kokokyinaka Asamoa ɔdi ne hene wɔ ne kwaeɛ mu. In his own forest the plantain-eater or clock bird is supreme, if nowhere else. *Every man wants to be king in his own castle.*
A canoe	Ɛhyɛn yɛka no afanu. The canoe must be paddled on both sides. *'Unity is strength.'*
A cockroach which has fallen among fowls	Tɛfrɛ atɔ nkokɔ mu, yɛdi no aprɛtoɔ. Fowls will not spare a cockroach that falls in their midst. *He who falls victim to his enemies can expect little mercy.*

Top Brass equipment for weighing gold dust, Akan traditional currency. It belongs to the treasury of the Ruler of the Akim Abuakwa State, Eastern Region, and comprises: scales (*nsania*), shovels for scooping up gold dust (*famfa*), spoons for lifting gold dust from the shovel and placing it on the scales (*saawa*), and boxes for storing gold dust (*abampruwa*). The spoons and boxes are engraved with beautiful geometrical designs. In the picture are also seen gold-weights in the forms of a padlock, a duiker standing on a cross-patée box, a hedgehog and a crocodile, and one of purely geometrical design.

Foot A brass casket, *kuduo*, of the Akwamuhene, Eastern Region. It is used as a container for gold dust and other valuables, and as a receptacle for ceremonial offerings. It has engraved decorations.

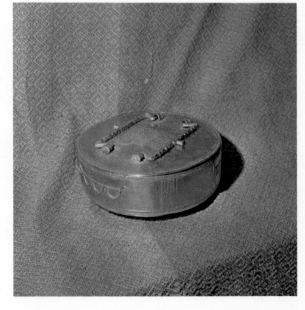

A Dagarti from Lawra, Northern Ghana, playing the xylophone. The gourds underneath the graduated hard-wood strips are of varying sizes and produce a wide range of sounds.

A set of *asɔkɔbɛn* or *asisibɛn*, 'talking' horns, belonging to the Ruler of the Akwapim State, Eastern Region, made out of ivory and decorated with beautiful leatherwork.

CHAPTER FOUR

Musical Instruments

A Christian missionary once observed that he considered that more hymns were sung in Ghana than anywhere else in Christendom. This obviously was meant to be a hyperbole but it is true, none the less, that he was describing a national characteristic which is as true of Ghanaians today as it was of their forebears of yesterday – the love of music. Song and dance are resorted to spontaneously in almost every phase of life: at work and play; on the battlefield and at festive celebrations; at birth and on reaching puberty; and at death.

The vocal music, such as the mournful duets of minstrels (*kwadwomfoɔ*), is highly interesting and no less significant in the social life of the people; but in a work on regalia, it is instrumental music and particularly the instruments themselves which must receive our primary attention. There is a wide variety of these instruments: idiophones or instruments of naturally resonant materials which vibrate through percussion – clappers, gongs, pellet-bells, xylophones, jingles and rattles; membranophones, i.e. all the varieties of drum; aerophones or wind instruments, such as horns, pipes or flutes; and chordophones or stringed instruments, which include lutes, musical bows, harps and violins.

These instruments are played alone or in combinations and are sometimes accompanied by singing or by recitations, half-sung and half-spoken. The drum, for example, used to summon an assembly is played alone; but the *kete* ensemble combines a variety of drums, a gong, rattle and the *durugya* flute. The latter is often played by itself in response to the recitations of minstrels.

Drums, flutes, horns, gongs and rattles are the most commonly used of these instruments.

Stringed instruments are found in Southern Ghana, and may have been quite popular in the past, as ceremonial instruments of this kind are to be seen among the regalia of chiefs – for example, the two golden lutes, *sika sankuo*, which form part of the special paraphernalia of the Golden Stool. But in modern times they are mostly used in Northern Ghana.

57

Ntahera horns of the Ruler of the Kwahu State, Eastern Region, being blown. They are made of ivory.

Musical Instruments

The use of musical instruments is socially controlled, some being restricted to chiefs, such as the *nkofe* horns, which may only be used by the Asantehene, and the *luginyini* horn, which is used exclusively in singing the praises of the head of the Dagomba State, the Ya Na, while the *kikaa* horn is used for the praises of his divisional chiefs. Also, in states where single instruments can be used by anybody, one may find ensembles of such instruments restricted. They may be the preserve of a chief or a privileged class of people. An instance is the *apirede* orchestra, made up of the *apirede* drum itself with the *apentemma* and *petia* drums, wooden clappers and gong. It is an ensemble for stool-carriers.

The same type of instruments or orchestras may be used on different occasions. The *adowa* orchestra, for instance, may play at a funeral but may also play on a joyful occasion, such as the installation ceremonies for a new chief. The repertoire of the instrument or orchestra and the accompanying song or dance-movement will, however, indicate what the occasion is.

Most of these instruments are used to provide music for the dance; but some are used for other purposes – providing rhythms for walking or working, giving signals or alarms, conveying messages, recounting the history of the people, reciting proverbs and wise sayings or singing the praises of rulers and distinguished persons. The castanet is used to punctuate the public utterances and coughs of the Nayiri. The Akan chief walks in state to the beat of the *mpintin* drums.

The *asuboa* drum imitates the cry of a crocodile and the *etwie* drum that of a leopard. The animals concerned may be the totem animals of the chiefs for whom the instruments are played, or the purpose of the imitation may be to convey that the rulers are regarded as being as powerful as the animal whose cries are imitated.

The *tatwea* horn of the Omanhene or head of the Asin Apimanim State in the Central Region imitates the bark of a dog (*ɔtwea*). It is said that in the past the sound of this horn announced that someone had been or was about to be executed. It was also meant to be a warning to the enemy on the battlefield that total annihilation of their troops was imminent. The dog, it is said, barked at anyone who approached it because it feared the man was bringing death to it. Hence the horn is also called *owuo* – death.

It is the musical instruments which 'talk' – those which convey messages, recount history, recite proverbs and wise sayings or sing praises – which have captivated and mystified the world. These are mostly horns, flutes and drums.

The principal horn of the Togbui or head of the Mafi State of Tongu in the Volta Region, the *kpega*, is such a horn, and makes the following reference to the migration of the Mafis from Nɔtsie in Togoland. (Almost all the Ewe states in the Volta Region allege that they migrated from Nɔtsie to escape the tyranny of its ruler.)

> *Anyigba, Anyigba, Anyigba*
> *Ne ènyam le Anyigba dzi hã la*
> *Anyigba dzi ko, manɔ*
> *Metsia tsitre.*

> Mighty land, mighty land,
> Send me away if you will.
> A dweller of some land shall I be still,
> From land can I never be banned.

To this the drum, *agblɔvu*, responds:

> *Tso, blu, Yeve, tso, blu, Yeve*
> *Ne mede megbe hã la le mele ava wɔm*
> *Nya le asinye, nya le asinye.*

> Stand up and shout *Yeve!*
> I retreat: but not to run away;
> There is a purpose to my flight.

The *atumpan* drums of the Akans are perhaps the best known of these 'talking' instruments. The body of the drum is carved out of the *tweneboa* or *tweneduro* tree (*Cordia millenii*). There are special carvers for this and it is taboo for the drummer to carve his own *atumpan*. The tense membrane or drum-head is made out of an elephant's ear and is stretched across the rim of the drum (*ɛyeɛ*) and held by a number of pegs, the *nsoa*, made from the wood of the *wɔbea* or *ɔfemma* tree (probably *Microdesmis puberula*), with a rope obtained from the fibre of the *bofunu* tree (probably *Haningana madagascariensis*).

The membrane is held tight or relaxed by hammering in or loosening the pegs. The hammering is done with a hammer which is often a small elephant's tusk. The regulation of the pegs helps to differ ntiate the tones of the drum.

60

Top A *durugya* flute of the Nsuta-hene, Ashanti. The flute itself is made of reed, *demire*, and its brush-like end, *afukaa*, of raffia. It is one of the instruments which 'speak', i.e. recount history and sing praises.

Foot Royal musicians of the Ya Na, Northern Ghana, playing a violin, *gorje*, and a rattle, *gagili*.

Musical Instruments

The *atumpan* are always found in pairs; one is known as the male (*atumpan nini*) and the other as the female (*atumpan bereɛ*). They give vowel sounds or high and low tones. Consonantal sounds are produced by a peapod-shaped piece of iron fixed to the tympanum of the male drum and called the *akasaa* – the speaker.

The drumsticks, *nkonta* or *ntwenta*, are obtained from a specially shaped branch of the *ɔfemma* tree (*Microdesmis puberula*). The handle is usually bound with cloth or wrapped round with *funtumia* rubber to prevent the drummer's hands from slipping. The drums, when being played, are propped against four bow-like sticks, the *nnyawa*, also made from the *ɔfemma* tree, to give the drums the correct angle.

Broadly speaking, the technique for making the *atumpan* drums, as described, holds good for other drums. The materials used and the form will of course differ from drum to drum. The *donno*, the hour-glass or squeeze drum, for example, commonly used throughout Ghana as a solo accompaniment to songs, and also in several drum ensembles, has a double membrane; both ends of its cylindrical body have a goatskin membrane stretched across them. The body is carved from the shea butter tree, *kraku*, which grows mostly in Northern Ghana.

The body of the *atumpan* drum is usually decorated with engraving directly on the wood or on beaten brass wrapped round the body. On ceremonial occasions the area round the pegs is swathed in a piece of white cloth which is presented by the chief for whom the drum is played. The two large, tall *bɔmmaa* drums of the *fɔntɔmfrɔm* orchestra are similarly wrapped on ceremonial occasions in a silk cloth given by the chief. The cloth marks the association of the chief with the drum. Other items of regalia, such as a *kuduo* or treasure-casket, are sometimes similarly wrapped.

Some drums are covered all over with felt cloth of various colours, and talisman decorations are hung from them. It was also fashionable in the past to decorate drums and horns with the skull, jaw-bones or limbs of defeated enemy warriors. The idea was to ridicule such persons. The *atumpan* drums were never given this kind of decoration.

Dr R. S. Rattray, in his book *Ashanti*, explains the mechanism of the speech music of the *atumpan*. He maintains that it is not based on any system of Morse code or signalling familiar to Europeans, but on an imitation by the drums of the sounds of words spoken by a human voice. This is done by copying the accent on a particular syllable, by stress or emphasis on a

Instruments of a *fɔntɔmfrɔm* orchestra of the Dormaahene, Brong-Ahafo, made up of a pair of *atumpan* or talking drums tilted and propped on three sticks, a pair of *bɔmmaa* drums in the background, three *twenesini* or short drums to the left of the *atumpan* and a pair of gongs to their right. All the drums except one of the *twenesini* have a decorative cover of *nsaa*, coarse blanket material. A *fɔntɔmfrɔm* orchestra provides music for dancing by men only.

A set of *twenesini*, short drums, of the *mmurukuwa* orchestra whose primary function traditionally was to provide the *abrafoɔ*, state executioners, with music for dancing. The two tall drums on either side of the picture are covered with cloth simulating leopard skin. The stuffed *abɔsodeɛ* or emblem decorating the front of the drum to the left represents the horns of a buffalo and is called *atweremmɛn*. The *abɔsodeɛ* of the drum to the right represents the state sword, *gyapatea*. Hanging above both *abɔsodeɛ* are talismans. The talismans and the *abɔsodeɛ* are covered in red felt. The drum in the centre has a felt cover in a red and black check. The set of instruments belongs to the Dormaahene, Brong-Ahafo.

63

Hausa musicians performing for the entertainment of an Akan ruler. The central figure is playing a trumpet and on his right is a player of the *donno* drum, found in most African communities.

Hausa players. The musician to the right of the picture is playing a trumpet. In most towns and villages in Ghana there is inevitably a Hausa community, and the members take part in durbars and other ceremonial festivities.

Mpintin drummers from Kumawu, Ashanti. The drums, decorated with leopard skin, comprise the long drum, *gyamadudu*, the rounded drum, *ntoa*, and the hourglass drum held under the armpit, *donno*. The orchestra provides the music to the rhythm of which a chief gracefully walks.

The *gulu* orchestra of the Navropio, Navrongo, Northern Ghana, made up of drums and flutes. Note that the long drums resemble the *gyamadudu* of the Akan *mpintin* orchestra and that there is also a *donno* drum.

particular word, by pauses, stops or punctuation, by the speed with which words or sentences are uttered and by gestures of the hands, arms, feet and head.

The speech imitation of the talking drums is facilitated by the fact that the Akan language is tonal, that is to say, the meaning of a word may depend on the tone or pitch at which the syllables of the word are spoken; and also by the fact that the Akan language is holophrastic – the words are better noted or understood in a sentence than standing by themselves.

The drums have set pieces or a number of holophrases, from which the drummer must not deviate if what he is drumming is to be understood by his hearers or even by his fellow-drummers.

The repertoire of the *atumpan* drums consists of expressions of condolence to the sources of the materials used for making the drums; references to creation; recitations of random proverbs, maxims and appellations; and narrations of the history of the drummer's state.

The sources of the drum materials, such as the *tweneboa* tree for the body of the drum and the *ɔfemma* tree for the drumsticks, are offered condolences because they were disturbed in order to obtain wood for the drum. In this connection, it must be noted that propitiatory offerings are made to them before they are cut to prevent their causing harm to the drummer.

On the drum they are given human names. Thus the *tweneboa* is referred to as *Tweneboa Kodua* and the *ɔfemma* as *Ɔfemma Kofi*, that is, Ɔfemma, the man born on a Friday.

An example of a reference to creation is the following:

> *Ɔdomankoma bɔɔ adeɛ, Borɔborɔ bɔɔ adeɛ*
> *Ɔbɔɔ kwan, ɔbɔɔ asuo, Ɔbɔɔ Akyerɛma*
> *Ɔkyere Kwawua ba brafo titire*
> *Yirefie Kwampon di abɔntenneɛ.*

When the Creator created the world, he created a path, the river, the drummer and finally man. Man, the mighty one, preyed on anything outside his abode.

One example of an appellative phrase – *Ababawa dua da ase a mmu, Akosua Dompo, mo a kurɔntɔ* – refers to a charming damsel who lies beneath a tree: she does so safely since, because of her great beauty, the tree will never fall on her.

66

CHAPTER FIVE

Personal Ornaments

Of the regalia of Ghanaian chiefs, particularly those of Southern Ghana, there is no part more distinctive than their ceremonial dress. The most notable item, of course, is the silk-woven, so-called *kente* cloth. A broad piece of woven cloth as a form of clothing or robe is not unknown among other communities, but the uniqueness of the *kente* lies not only in the artistry of its manufacture but also in the manner in which it is worn and the regal dignity it confers on the wearer.

The main body-garment is obviously the distinctive feature of a chief in full dress, but ornaments for the other parts of the body, head, feet, neck and fingers, are of no less interest and attraction. 'Personal Ornaments', the title of this chapter, is therefore to be understood as including all these other items of dress.

Personal ornaments in Southern Ghana are to receive greater attention, not only because they are made out of more precious materials and are richer in ornamentation and variety, but also because they are, as already said, more distinctive than those of the north, which show predominantly Islamic influence and are similar to the costume one comes across elsewhere, as in Northern Nigeria. The robes of the south, nevertheless, are not entirely free of Islamic influence and some of them are actually identical to or have evolved from their equivalents in the north, such as the talisman-decorated smocks and caps.

ROBES

The ceremonial robes of Northern Ghana rulers comprise a variety of gowns or flowing garments, two or more of which are worn at the same time, reminding one of the layers of vestments which are worn by a Catholic bishop at a Pontifical High Mass. They are made out of various kinds of material: imported cotton, linen and silk, and locally woven wool. Some are plain, in particular those worn as inner garments; others, especially the outer garments or cloaks, have richly coloured patterns and

67

embroideries. The woven wool, called *fuugu*, is usually used for tunics or smocks, some of which are ornamented with decorative talismans.

In Southern Ghana also, *fuugu* smocks, apparently obtained from the north, have long been used by chiefs, mostly on the battlefield and for funerals. Some of these chiefs have a principal smock, called *batakarikɛseɛ*, which they wear at the commencement of their installation rites. The installation, at which the chief promises to be faithful to his people, is considered a solemn occasion, as much so as going to war, hence the use of the smock. It has become fashionable in contemporary Ghana for politicians to don a *batakari* when they want to appeal to their followers on some grave national issue.

.The *batakari*, however, as far as Southern Ghana is concerned, is only one of some five different types of garment which are worn on mournful or solemn·occasions, the others being *kuntunkuni*, *kɔbene*, *birisi*, *hyewo-a-ɛnhye*, *nkrawoɔ* and *nwɔmu*. All these together are classed as *akonin ntoma* – 'cloth for the valiant heart'.

The *kuntunkuni*, *kɔbene* and *birisi*, of darkish brown, reddish or russet-brown, and black respectively, are dyed cloths, the dyes being obtained from the bark of a tree, for example, *Bombax brericuspe*, or from·clay of the appropriate colour, such as *ntwoma*.

The original fabric is either a native-woven cloth or an imported cotton or linen, usually of a plain white colour. After the dyeing, the cloth may also be stamped with what have come to be known as *adinkra* stamps or prints. A cloth thus stamped may be called an *adinkra* or *ntiamu*. The *kɔbene*, which is worn when a close relative dies or when there is some national calamity, is never stamped; for a stamped cloth, although it can be a mourning cloth, is also worn when one wants to appear smart.

The stamps used for the *adinkra* patterns are made out of fragments of old calabashes. These are dipped in a vegetable liquid obtained from the bark of the *badɛ* tree. The cloth is pegged taut on the ground for the stamping. There are no fewer than fifty different kinds of these calabash stamps in regular use.

Some of the patterns are mere geometrical designs, such as concentric circles, chequer-boards and lozenges, called respectively *adinkra panin*, *nframadan* and *nhwemu*. Some are actual or stylized representations of inanimate objects, plants and animals, while others are abstract symbols of proverbs. Of actual representational designs there are, for instance, the *donno* drum, a heart, the hair-style of attendants to a queen mother, and a

The Ruler of the State of Sefwi Wiawso, Western Region, in a
military *batakarikɛsɛ* smock with a corresponding hat and holding
a club ornamented with leopard skin and felt. Sewn to the smock
are talismans, also containers for gunpowder and two white horse-
tail whisks.

A Queen Mother, Western Region, adorned with precious beads and with a hair-style typical of the Fanti, a section of the Akan-speaking peoples. She is dancing at a state festival.

Fanti women, Western Region, displaying a variety of hair-styles.

Maltese cross, these designs being called respectively *donno*, *akoma*, *nkotimsofoɔ-puaa* (another form of swastika), and *mmusuyideɛ* (literally, that which drives away evil spirits).

Examples of stylized representations, most of which also symbolize sayings, are those of the *aya* leaf of fern, the horns of a ram, the so-called 'little eyes' of the king and the toucan bird with the beak turned backwards; these designs are called respectively *aya* (signifying fearlessness and independence), *dwennimɛn* (referring to the proverb that when the horns of two rams clash in a fight, one must give way to the other, a symbol of strength), *ɔhene aniwa* (to have the favour of the king), and *tɔakyireɛfa* (one should not ignore one's past; or, past experience must be a guide for one's future). Abstract symbols include *obi nka obi kwa* (no one bites or offends another without some reason); *mate-masie* (what I have heard I have kept or will ponder on); *Gye-Nyame* or *kyerɛ-nyame* (one must dread God alone; or, only God has power to prosper or destroy).

The *adinkra* patterns are said to have been copied from the carved designs on the *sɛkyɛdua* or column of the Stool of Adinkra, who was ruler of the Gyaman State (now in the Ivory Coast) about the beginning of the nineteenth century – hence the name. A replica of this stool, made in the days of Adinkra, is to be found in the Prempeh II Jubilee Museum, Kumasi. These designs, however, may be yet another example of Islamic influence on Ghana culture as they may originally have been amulet signs or symbols, perhaps of the Tuareg Arabs.

Hyewo-a-ɛnhye (I burn but do not burn – i.e. it is fire-proof) is also a robe of Islamic inspiration, more directly so than the *adinkra*. It is a cloth of white calico printed with some writings from the Koran. It is usually worn by the chief on the day when he is to pronounce judgment in a court case. The robe, with its accompanying cap decorated with talismans or a headband of cowries, is believed to be able to neutralize any charm that either party to the suit may have brought to the court to tilt the judgment in his favour.

Nkrawoɔ is a garment made of felt cloth of any colour, but usually of red, and has appliqué and embroidered decorations which are symbolic. The appliqué designs depend on the fancy of the craftsman; but the more usual ones are *kontonkurowi* or concentric circles, the moon and stars, or birds and animals, such as the plantain-eater, crocodile and elephant.

Nwɔmu is a broad piece of imported silk or linen material into which are woven in horizontal lines narrow strips of satin-stitch embroidery, having

Above

A crown and two hats of the Ruler of the Manya Krobo State, Eastern Region. The crown, in the centre of the picture, is entirely made of gold filigree. It is hexagonal, and the six sides, representing the six clans of the state, are detachable. On each side, at the point of intersection of four lines, is a palm-tree flower. This symbolizes the source of life. The points where the sides are hooked together are surmounted by exquisite representations of palm leaves, symbolizing triumph. On top of the crown is a gold cast of an eagle, the totem of the state and the symbol of strength.

The hat on the right is made of leopard skin decorated with golden parrot feathers, symbolizing bravery. Between the feathers are gilded medicine gourds and in front is the coat of arms of the state wrought in gold – a wreath, a miniature crown and a boss symbolizing wisdom. Like the filigree crown this hat is topped by a gold eagle. The hat is modelled on that of a chief priest, for in the past the Ruler of the state was also regarded as a 'Pontifex Maximus'.

The hat on the left is designed to represent a lion crouching in the Krobo Hills that surround the state. The top is made of leopard skin and the lower part of that of a lion. (See p. 82.)

Opposite

Top   Three hats of the Akroponghene, Ruler of the Akwapim State, Eastern Region. That on the left is made of sheepskin, that in the centre of velvet, and they both have embossed gold decorations. The hat on the right is made of embroidered cloth decorated with pieces of leopard skin and talismans. The rectangular embossed gold decorations are of the talisman design, *sɛbɛ*, the circular one of the spider design, *ananse*.

Centre   Three crowns of the Ruler of the Akim Kotoku State, Eastern Region; two made of leopard skin and surmounted by a gold cast of a parrot, and the third of duiker skin and surmounted by a crouching lion. The gold ornaments include shells, stars and the *aya* leaf.

Foot   Head bands or fillets of the Ruler of the Akrokerri State, Ashanti. This type of head-dress is the one generally worn by Akan rulers on ceremonial occasions. They are made of fine velvet and richly decorated with gold ornaments – shells, stars, crescents, crosses and talismans.

73

the same appearance as the weft pattern of a *kente*. The spaces between these strips or *kente* ribbons are equal, and they are sometimes stamped with *adinkra* designs. The ribbons may have straight edges or may be notched or saw-edged; the two types are called respectively *kukruboɔ* and *kaw*.

Both the *nkrawoɔ* and *nwɔmu* are worn, not necessarily but usually, for solemn occasions, such as when the chief, being in mourning, has to turn out for a festive occasion. They are sometimes made in colours that can only be used at times of festivity.

The *kente* too is a festal cloth and more popularly used as such than any other. It is woven in narrow strips (*ntomaban*), approximately four inches in width, on traditional looms (*nsadua*). The strips are later sewn together to form the whole cloth. Four different kinds of weave or pattern can be distinguished in a strip, which together give the cloth a chequered design, namely, the *adwini*, *akyɛm*, *ahwepan*, and *nkyeretire* or *nkyereano*.

The *adwini* or warp designs are the principal and most ornamental of the weaves and are flanked on either side by the *akyɛm*, which are in turn followed by the weft designs, *ahwepan*, plain horizontal lines which stand at right angles to the *adwini* and the *akyɛm*. At both ends of the strip are the *nkyeretire* or *nkyereano*, which are two or three combinations of *adwini* with corresponding *akyɛm* but without any *ahwepan*. The exclusion of the *ahwepan* gives the *nykeretire* a rich concentration of colour and design and it is the most expensive part of the cloth. In Ashanti in the past the width of the *nkyeretire* was controlled by social tradition, no one being allowed to have the same width as the Asantehene. The *adwiniasa*, considered the richest and loveliest of *kente* cloths – hence the name, which means the exhaustion of all designs – is made of *adwini* and *akyɛm* patterns only.

The *adwini* designs are given their own names, such as *fa-hia kɔtwere Agyeman* (rest your poverty on Agyeman – referring to one of the kings of Ashanti who was known to be particularly kind to those in need); *esaani* (the eyes of a caterpillar); and *nkyinkyim* (referring to curves, coils or spirals). But it is by the name of the *ahwepan* or weft design that the cloth as a whole is known. Instances are numerous, but it will suffice to refer to *ɛfoɔdua* (the tail of a colebus monkey); *Amponsem* (named after one of the past kings of the Denkyira State who reigned about the latter part of the seventeenth century); *dokuasin-anwomfoɔ-mu* (so expensive that the poor are unable to buy); *bɔbɔserewa* (not being serious); and *ɔyokomman* (the oldest of these designs, named after the *oyoko* clan).

74

Top Nana Aburam Akpandja III, Ruler of the Buem State wearing a multi-coloured *konin* cloth.

Foot Helmets, *yugongo*, made of sliced calabashes decorated with cowries, horse-tails and leatherwork, and crowned with the horns of a cow, buffalo or water-buck. They belong to the Navropio, Northern Ghana, and in the past were worn on the battle-field. They are now mostly worn by the bodyguard and musicians of the Navropio.

The names of these designs emerge from the fertile imagination of the weavers. There appear to be no limitations to the scope of this imagination; one could say that their achievement is only paralleled by those responsible for the naming of racehorses. A weaver has the prerogative of naming a new design which he has invented, and these inventions are being made continually, by the introduction of completely new designs or by the rearrangement of the colours of old ones. A recent design is named *Fatia fata Nkrumah* (the good wife of the President of Ghana deserves her husband). Generally speaking, any design can be worn by anybody, at any time; but in Ashanti one comes across stringent restrictions on the designs that a weaver can sell to his customers, some of which are still obeyed in spite of the allurement of cash profits. One such restricted design is the *ɔhye-gya* (the consumer of fire), which is the first *kente* to be woven for the Asantehene on his accession to the Golden Stool, and that which at death is spread on his corpse when lying in state.

The art of weaving in Ghana was first practised by the peoples of the north and is said to have been introduced into Ashanti by one Otaa Kraban, an Ashanti from Bonwire, the village best known in Ghana for the making of *kente* cloth. He studied the art at Salaga which was famous for the manufacture of the *fuugu* woven cloth, from the Fulani, who made coarse blankets known as *nsaa*, and also from the people of Gyaman in the Ivory Coast. From Ashanti the art spread to the littoral. Before the introduction of weaving in the south, the people used bark cloth obtained from the bark of the tree *kyɛnkyɛn (Antiaris africana)*.

Otaa Kraban experimented with his newly discovered art, using raffia as material for the woven cloth. The result looked like the weave of a basket and so was called *kɛntɛn* or *kɛntɛn toma* (the basket cloth). Raffia was in time replaced by cotton spun from the cotton grown in the country, particularly in the north. In the past women were forbidden to weave; it was taboo for them even to touch a loom or speak directly to their weaver-husbands during their menstrual period. But women were almost exclusively responsible for picking and spinning the cotton.

The cotton was sometimes dyed with the juice of certain plants to obtain threads of different colours, such as black, *bibire* or *mmre*, from the juice of *tatwee*; blue, *hoa*, from *akaseɛ*; and red, *koogyan*, from *daagyere*.

It was soon discovered that the *kente* could also be made of silk material made out of the long silky yarns produced by a species of spider, *ɔkɔmantan*.

A cap of eagle feathers which forms part of the ceremonial dress of the bearer of the *mpomponsuo* sword, Akwamu, Eastern Region. In front of it are gold ram's horns, talismans and a leopard-skin band.

A hat of the Ruler of the Ahanta (Busua) State, Western Region, made of skin and covered with gold decorations. These show various symbols such as a crocodile, an elephant and a palm tree.

Precious *aggrey* beads and gold-encrusted sandals of the Ruler of the Akim Abuakwa State, Eastern Region. The sandals have shell and talisman decorations.

The yarns thus obtained, like the cotton thread, were dyed with the juice of plants. With the importation of silk fabrics by European merchants, these were purchased, unravelled and re-woven into *kente*. T. E. Bowdich, in his account of his *Mission from Cape Coast Castle to Ashantee* of 1817, wrote, 'The caboceers [headmen] wove Ashantee cloths of extravagant price, from the costly foreign silks which had been unravelled to weave them in all varieties of colour as well as pattern.'

The raffia *kente* of Otaa Kraban was plain, without any designs, and so was the cotton *kente* immediately following. When, later, designs were woven into the fabric and threads of different colours were used, a distinction was made between the plain and the patterned cloth, the name of *kente* being retained for the former, the latter being called *nkyeremu*. This distinction led to the recognition of two classes of weavers, the *kentefoo* and the *nkyeremufoo*. *Kente* is nowadays used indiscriminately for any kind of woven cloth, but the proper term that covers all kinds of woven cloth is *nwontoma* (the woven cloth).

Cloths, beaten, printed, embroidered or woven locally, do not by any means exhaust the chief's store of garments. There is a large, if not a greater, percentage of imported cloths which are given local names but are seldom, if ever, used for ceremonial occasions. They include velvets (*ago*) and silks (*serekye*) of brocade and damask weaves, particular patterns having their own names, such as *dua-wusu*, *akokɔbaatan akyi* and *nankanini-akyi*; cotton textiles of different kinds or patterns, for example, *daano* with block-printed patterns, *madras* of chequered design, presumably imported from Madras in India, *mmoraa toma*, a light-weight textile, and fake or machine-produced imitations of locally woven and printed cloths.

Other items of clothing include the loincloth, tunic, head-dress, sandals and jewellery. The more traditional form of loincloth is the *danta*, usually made of locally manufactured or imported silk and tied round the loins in certain complicated turns and twists. Later developments of the *danta* are the *toga* and *pieto*, which are types of knickerbocker. The ordinary form of European short trouser is also worn. The tunic, made of silk or linen, is used mostly by chiefs on the littoral.

HEAD-DRESS

There are two categories of head-dress, *ɛkyɛ*, comprising caps, hats, helmets and crowns, and *abotire*, which includes headbands or fillets and turbans.

Skullcaps. *krɔbɔnkyɛ*, of the Ruler of the Kumawu State, Ashanti. They are made of duiker skin and decorated with talismans, the leaves of a pepper plant and designs such as the spider design, *ananse*. One is surmounted by a pineapple plant cast in gold, another by a fruit with a strong perfume called *prekɛsɛ*. These caps are worn on solemn occasions such as a funeral or an installation ceremony.

Silver pendant talismans on a necklace of the Ruler of the Wa State in Northern Ghana. They are beautifully engraved with geometrical designs and two of them with palm trees.

79

Rings, bangles, necklaces, anklets and a horse-tail switch with a gold handle, belonging to the Ruler of the Akrokerri State, Ashanti.

Precious *aggrey* beads of the Ruler of the Agona Nyakrom State, Western Region. The materials for some are mined locally, others are believed to be of Phoenician origin.

80

A cap is made of cotton, silk, velvet or locally woven cloth, sometimes of the same material as that used for a tunic or smock, and the two are worn together. The locally woven cloth is usually the Northern Ghana *fuugu* cloth, to which reference has already been made in this chapter. The cap, like the tunic, is decorated with talismans, which are sometimes embossed with gold or silver leaf. It is referred to as *kabisakyɛ* (the cap of *kabisa*, the fetish from whom the talismans were originally obtained).

Caps, as described above, are most commonly worn in the north; this is in keeping with the northern ties with the Moslem faith and manner of dress generally. Here the caps are made of a variety of decorative materials and used for joyful ceremonial occasions. In the south, however, hardly any form of cap is used apart from the *kabisakyɛ*, which is worn with the *batakari* tunic for mourning and other solemn occasions. The Ewes in the south have a distinctive type of cap made of knitted wool, *togbenya*.

Of the type of head-dress which the people call *ɛkyɛ*, I have classified those made of cloth as caps. The basic material of some crowns is also cloth, principally velvet, but a crown is more like a hat than a cap. On the other hand, *krɔbɔnkyɛ*, a hat made of animal skin and worn at the back of the head, is more properly described as a skullcap than a hat because of its appearance.

Hats are made chiefly of the hide of certain animals, such as the colebus monkey, duiker, leopard, tiger, lion and elephant. Some have silver or gold decorations, particularly those of privileged chiefs, and others have attached to them charms or talismans, cowries and feathers. The animal whose skin is used may have some special significance in the history, mythology or religion of the people. Like the skins used in the north as thrones, the hide may also denote the status of the chief who wears the hat. The *dɛnkyɛmkyɛ* of the Asantehene was made by King Osei Tutu, the virtual founder of the Ashanti Kingdom, out of the skins of an elephant, a ram, a leopard and a toucan he encountered on his journey from Akwamu to Kumasi when he was invited to succeed his uncle as King of Ashanti in the late seventeenth century. The *dɛnkyɛmkyɛ* was so called because it was worn by a ruler then accepted as the most powerful of his people. To this day, anyone who makes empty or undeserved boasts of greatness or might is reminded that he is not the wearer of the *dɛnkyɛmkyɛ*.

Helmet-like hats are to be found in the Northern Region, for example, the *yugongo* of the Navropio. These are made of the sliced halves of

81

calabashes and are decorated with cowries and skins. They have tops made of the horns of certain animals, such as the cow, buffalo and waterbuck. They were originally used by the ruler and his men on the battlefield but are now chiefly worn by his bodyguard and musicians.

Crowns of the form used by European monarchs were unknown in Ghana in traditional times. Hats of skins, with silver or gold decorations of some historical or symbolic significance, served the purposes of a crown and were used by the ruler on solemn occasions, for example, at his installation rites. An instance is a boat-shaped hat belonging to the ruler of the Manya Krobo State, Eastern Region, designed to represent a crouching lion in the Krobo Hills which surround the state. It is made in two parts, the material having been taken from hats worn by former rulers of the state. The top part is made out of the skin of a leopard and the lower part from that of a lion, both of which animals at different times had haunted the capital of the state but were eventually heroically slain. It has decorations of three feathers symbolizing valour, gilt talismans representing those which adorn the original hats, a badge showing an eagle (the totem of the state), and palm leaves denoting the state's victories on the battlefield.

In modern times, however, some chiefs on the littoral have made crowns which look like imitations of European crowns but are given decorations and names of local significance. The body is usually made of velvet but there are instances of the entire crown being made of repoussé or filigreed gold.

Of the second category of head-dress, *abotire*, the turban, was perhaps the first to be used, and the headband or fillet may have been a development from it. It was originally simply a piece of the same kind of cloth as was used for a garment, tied round the head. The headband usually matches the garment with which it is worn but is not now necessarily of the same material. The band, about an inch in width, is usually of velvet studded with gold decorations – talismans, cowries, shells, groundnut leaves, stars, crescents, crosses and *aya* leaves of fern. Also sometimes used as a headband is a string (*tipaeɛ-sɛbɛ* – so called because it is meant to be a cure for headaches), from which are hung talismans.

Among the Akan-speaking peoples, it is usual to find a link between the principal ceremonial sword of state and the hat which serves as the crown of the ruler. The two may have been worn together by the founder of the state when hunting. The hat is therefore worn on ceremonial occasions by

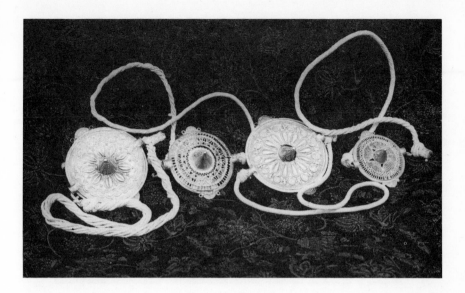

A pair of gold breastplates, *akrafokonmu*. Each is made up of two plates strung to white cords. They are worn by the 'soul washers', the officials responsible for the 'soul washing' ceremonies of the Ruler of the Berekum State, Brong-Ahafo.

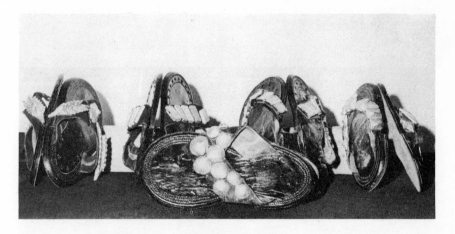

Five pairs of sandals, heirlooms of the Ruler of the Mampong State, Ashanti. The straps have gold decorations such as shells and talismans.

83

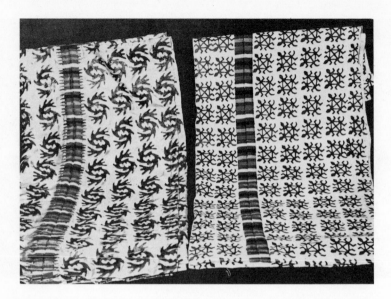

Examples of the two kinds of *nwɔmu* cloth in the Prempeh II Jubilee Museum, Kumasi. One has a straight-edged *kente* band or ribbon running through it, *kukrubɔɔ*; the other a saw-edged *kente* band, *kaw*. The *kukrubɔɔ* has an *adinkra* pattern print of a stylized version of the gold-weight representing two crocodiles with a common stomach (see p. 48); the *adinkra* print of the *kaw* is an abstract representation of the saying '*Obi nka obi kwa*' (I offend no one without a reason).

Two examples of *kente* cloth in the Prempeh II Jubilee Museum, Kumasi. The more richly decorated, with a profusion of zigzag and lozenge patterns, is called the *adwiniasa* (the exhaustion of all designs). The other is called *abrewaben* (the clever old lady).

the custodian of the sword and is used by the ruler only at his installation. The custodians of the other swords of state also have their appropriate hats; the one most commonly found throughout the Akan states is that of the custodian of the *mpomponsuo* sword, which is made of eagle feathers and ornamented with gold decorations. Other state officials such as the bodyguard, *atumtofoɔ*, and the court-criers, *nsɛneɛfoɔ*, have similar hats.

SANDALS

One cannot fail to be struck by the apparent oddity of a chief in Northern Ghana dressed in his colourful traditional robes but wearing a pair of European-made riding boots. The explanation is that on ceremonial occasions chiefs of that region usually appear on horseback. The proper footwear for them, as well as for chiefs of Southern Ghana, consists of richly ornamented, traditional sandals.

Sandals in their present form have gradually evolved from something much cruder. Originally they were made out of the bark of the silk-cotton tree, *onyina* (*Ceiba pentandra*) and had a strap of cane. The appearance of their footwear was of no interest to the people; as a mainly nomadic people they were chiefly concerned with having good protection for their feet on their peregrinations. Later some care was taken to have the bark nicely shaped. This required soft wood and so the bark of *Funtumia elastica*, *sennuro* (*Alstonia boonei*) and *odwuma* (corkwood- or umbrella-tree, *Musanga cecropioides*) was used. This type of sandal, rather like the wooden shoes worn in Holland, was called *nkuronnua*.

With the process of time, bark was replaced by hide, particularly by cowhide. Three types of sandal have evolved consecutively, *kyaw-kyaw*, *mpaboatraa* and *mpaboapa*, the first being light-weight and the succeeding ones having an increasing number of layers of hide. The *mpaboapa* are the ones now used, and the chiefs who are privileged to do so adorn the strap with silver or gold decorations, the same as those used for headbands, *abotire*.

It is a taboo for a chief to walk barefoot; if he does, it is believed that he will precipitate a famine. When the deposition of a chief is declared, one of the first symbolic acts is to remove his sandals and force him to walk away barefoot. At the same time his stool is removed from the public meeting-place where he is declared destooled or deposed.

JEWELLERY

To complete the list of the personal ornaments of Ghanaian chiefs, one must also mention their jewellery which includes neck-wear (*ayanneɛ*), elbow-wear (*bafurum-sɛbɛ*), knee-wear (*nantuo* or *nananim suman*) and ankle-wear (*aberempɔnnaaseɛ*). These are made of wrought or repoussé gold, precious beads, sometimes interspersed with gold nuggets, and talismans (*suman* and *sɛbɛ*), sometimes adorned with silver or gold leaf.

Top The gold-plated ornament is a pendant for a necklace of gold, red and green cord, called *ayanneɛ*. Surrounding it are other gold necklaces, *asaadeɛ*, which are worn cross-wise over the chest. They all belong to the Denkyira-hene, Central Region.

Foot Fly-whisks of the Denkyirahene, Central Region. The one in the centre is made from an elephant's tail and has a leather handle. The other two are made from horse-tails; the handle of one is covered with red felt and the other is gold-plated. Fly-whisks are used by practically all chiefs in Ghana ɛs part of their ceremonial dress; but in Denkyira the King's messengers carry them as badges of credence.

The black stools of the Ruler of the Mampong State, Ashanti, resting on a bed. The middle one is that of the founder of the state, Nana Amaniampong. In front of the bed are a pair of wine vessels, *brɔtoa*, an imported silver bowl, a bag, *sannaa*, containing gold dust, gold-weights and the apparatus for weighing the dust. Lying on the *sannaa* is a sword which protects the stools.

Silver-encrusted ceremonial stools of the Ruler of the Kumawu State, Ashanti, resting on an *akonkromfi* chair and a *hwedɔm* chair. In the foreground are two imported silver vessels and two silver-encrusted calabashes. The vessels and calabashes are used for the feeding of the stools.

CHAPTER SIX

Other Regalia

This chapter consists of a number of brief notes on such regalia as have not been classified in any of the foregoing chapters. This could amount to almost as much as has already been written if it were to do justice to all the appurtenances to the office of a Ghanaian chief. Pots and pans of the royal kitchen, equipment for the bath and receptacles for food, wine and water, all properly belong to the royal inheritance. The intention, however, is to deal here only with the major items not already mentioned, particularly those which are in use when a chief appears in state: umbrellas, palanquins and maces or staffs of office carried by linguists or spokesmen.

UMBRELLAS

Umbrellas, or rather state umbrellas, to distinguish them from the ordinary article, are used by chiefs in all parts of Ghana as canopies and as another symbol of their office. The idea of such a canopy naturally originated from the use of an ordinary umbrella or sunshade as protection against rain and sun.

Before European-made umbrellas were known, the broad leaves of certain kinds of plants, such as *anworomo, nkonkuro, borɔdeɛ* and *mankani*, sometimes hoisted on a stick, were used to cover the head. Out of this primitive type of umbrella was developed the flat-topped kind of state umbrella, the *katamanso*. Another type, the *bankyiniiɛ*, with a convex top, is based on the European umbrella and the third type, *akuromponkyiniwa*, is like the *bankyiniiɛ* but smaller in size. The latter is for everyday use, the other two for ceremonial occasions. It is claimed in Kumawu in Ashanti that the *bankyiniiɛ* is so called because that type of umbrella was originally used to cover copper statues of a mother with her three children, the *Abamo* statues which seem to smile or frown according to how they are looked at. The statues and umbrella were captured from one Ataadafiram from the Volta Region by the Kumawus in the late seventeenth century. The derivation of *bankyiniiɛ* is said to be from *kyiniiɛ* of *bamo* (*abamo* with the initial *a* elided).

89

Top   Gold-plated staffs of office of the Techimanhene's linguists (Brong-Ahafo) with the following symbolic tops (*left* to *right*):

(*a*) A snail, a tortoise and a hunter holding a gun – to illustrate the saying that if it were only for the snail and the tortoise there would be no guns in the forest (snails and tortoises are picked up and so it is not necessary to fire).

(*b*) Two men seated; one eats from a dish and the other looks on – to symbolize the proverb that a prepared meal belongs to the one who has paid for it and not to the one who is hungry.

(*c*) *Sika putuo*, a stack for keeping gold dust in cans – to call attention to the wealth of the state.

Foot   A group of state umbrellas of the Akroponghene, Eastern Region, made of silk, felt and velvet in brilliant colours.

The large ceremonial umbrellas are manufactured locally from different kinds of beautifully coloured textiles: silk, felt, brocade, damask and *kente*. The *akuromponkyiniwa*, usually made of plain black linen, is mostly imported; but it is sometimes made locally of different materials like the others.

On the top of the umbrella is usually placed a carved symbol (*ntuatire*) of some saying or message, wrapped in silver or gold leaf like the *abɔsodeɛ* of a state sword. The umbrella is usually named after this symbolic top; for example, the top of the *abɛtene* of the Berekumhene in the Brong-Ahafo Region is the crest of a palm tree, illustrating the saying, *nnua nyinaa bɛwoso a, ɛnyɛ abɛ* (all trees may shed their leaves at one time or another, but not the palm tree).

The Asantehene has no fewer than twenty-three different umbrellas, each of which is used on a particular occasion. The *akokɔtan* or *akokɔbaatan*, which has a top representing a hen with her chicken, is used when he presides over a case in which an attempt is made to settle differences between two chiefs or a chief and his subjects in a peaceful manner.

PALANQUINS

An English soldier who saw a palanquin for the first time called it a stretcher on which Ghana chiefs rode. J. G. Christaller in his *Dictionary of the Asante and Fante Language* defines it as 'a long basket in which kings or chiefs are carried'. The word palanquin will, indeed, sound strange to many readers, but it is the name that the British have given to *apakan*, a kind of litter or hammock in which chiefs of Southern Ghana are carried when they appear in state, the substitute for a state coach in Europe or a horse in Northern Ghana, which serves the same function as the sedan-chair, once widely used in Europe.

Before *apakan* came to be used, a chief was carried on the shoulders of one of his subjects, such a method being then called *akɔnkɔn*. Later the chief sat on the joined hands of two subjects; this method was known as *nkonta*. The idea of a palanquin was conceived from the use of cane baskets, variously known as *ɛyeɛ*, *demmire* and *borɔkena*, for carrying farm products, and particularly from *pankase*, another cane carrier, used for conveying corpses.

There are two kinds of palanquin. The *apakantene*, the older form, is now used by minor chiefs and is borne by two persons. It is suspended on a single pole. The other is *epie*, suspended on two poles, also called *nnuanan*, because it is borne by four persons, and *denkyedenkye*, because it rocks while being carried.

Chiefs who are privileged to do so decorate the outside of their palanquins with felt cloth and leopard skin. The inside is covered with *nsaa*, a coarse blanket, and there are two cushions, one for a seat and the other for a back-rest. As the chief sits in the palanquin, he is canopied under one or two of the state umbrellas; sword-bearers, who walk alongside, rest the hilts of their swords on the edges of the palanquin. It is usual for a chief seated in a palanquin to be followed by drummers, to whose music he dances on the palanquin, sometimes with a gun and a sword in his hands. The carriers of the state umbrellas make them flutter to the rhythm of the music. Some chiefs on the littoral, for example, in Akwapim, have their *Ɔkra*, a young child who represents the chief's soul, with them in the palanquin.

A queen mother has a special kind of litter, all of wood, called *sako*.

LINGUIST-STICKS OR STAFFS OF OFFICE

Linguist is the name given to *ɔkyeame*, a member of the class of elders through whom an Akan chief speaks and is spoken to at both public and private meetings. He is the mouthpiece or spokesman of the chief. Other ethnic groups have a similar office in their political or constitutional set-up. Linguists also have other duties. They advise on traditional law and custom, being regarded as experts in these matters; they are sent as ambassadors to other states to declare war, negotiate for peace or convey some important message; they act as chiefs of protocol for visiting potentates; in courts of law they pronounce judgment on behalf of the chief; and at ritual ceremonies they are present to support the chief in the offering of prayers.

The *ɔkyeame* thus holds a very important office in the state and it is said that it depends on him whether a state stands or falls. He is made the ruler of a village or a number of villages within the state. His status is nevertheless inferior to that of the head of the state and his elders. A saying has it that it is an ill omen if the linguist appears to be like the chief himself. His office is denoted by a staff or mace, called the *akyeame poma*.

The staff is of wood and privileged chiefs wrap their linguists' staves with silver or gold leaf. It is usual for a staff to have a symbolic emblem affixed to the top like that of state umbrellas. These tops depict sayings or

A two-tiered umbrella called *Obi da obi so*, meaning everyone inevitably has a superior in some respect. The umbrella, which belongs to the Ruler of the Sefwi State, Western Region, has a top, *ntuatire*, of an *akofena*, a sword for fighting.

A group of umbrella tops, *ntuatire*:
(a) The knotted stem of a cane plant, *babadua*, indicating the saying that a vigilant chief will surely detect any plots hatched against him.
(b) An *anomawerɛmfoɔ* bird – the bird that is so powerful that it takes bullets to kill it. That is why the bird has kegs of gunpowder in its mouth and on its wings.
(c) A hand holding an *akofena*, a fighting sword.
(d) A stool lying on its side.
(e) A fist with the thumb pointing skywards to signify that only God matters.
(f) An urn, *kuduo*, containing charms and resting on a stool.

93

Gilded staffs of office of the linguists of the Berekumhene, Brong-Ahafo. They have the following symbolic tops:

(a) A lion trampling on a hunter and holding his gun in its mouth. There are also two snails climbing to the top of the staff. The meaning is that if the lion is able to defy even the hunter with his gun, the snail is no problem.

(b) An eagle having caught a cobra and trampling on a gun. There is nothing left in the bush of which it can be afraid.

(c) A buffalo, the totem of the stool and royal lineage of the Berekum State. It is regarded as the most powerful animal after the lion.

(d) A cockerel and a hen illustrating the proverb 'Akokɔ bedeε nim adekyeε, nanso otie no akokonini ano' – the hen knows when it is dawn but leaves it to the cockerel to announce it.

(e) A cooking pot on a hearth and the head of a chicken on the lid, symbolizing the saying 'Aboa tiri enyera nkwan mu' – one cannot mistake a head of a bird in the soup even if the other parts of the bird are unrecognizable.

Three long swords, *afenatene*, and five linguists' staffs of office. Their symbolic tops are as follows (*left* to *right*):

(*a*) A hen stepping over her chicks. This symbolizes the saying that if a hen steps on her chicks, it is not to punish them but to keep them together and to prevent them being trampled by someone else. The symbol signifies the love and duty a mother owes to her children. The symbol is known as *Akokobaatan ne ne mma*, the mother and children.

(*b*) An egg held in a human hand, signifying the saying that to hold responsible office is like holding an egg in the hand.

(*c*) A snail, a gun and a tortoise (see top colour plate, p. 90).

(*d*) A lad holding a spear and stroking a lion. Only youths who have not learnt of a lion's fierceness can attempt to play with it or aim to kill it with a spear.

(*e*) A chief sitting on a stool to pour a libation.

proverbs, or represent historical incidents or certain qualities which the ruler is supposed to possess. A popular top is a human hand holding an egg, reminding the ruler before whom the staff is borne by one of his linguists, that to be a ruler is like holding an egg in the hand: if it is pressed too hard it breaks; but if not held tightly enough it may slip and smash on the ground. The staff held by the Asantehene's chief linguist is called *Asɛm-patia*, meaning that true evidence given in court is always short.

When dealing with clubs in Chapter Two, I expressed the opinion that linguist-sticks may have originated from clubs used by chiefs in the past as a fighting and defensive weapon. The proverb *patafoɔ di abaa* (he who tries to settle a quarrel runs the risk of being beaten with the stick) appears to be a reminder of this early stage of the people's history. This surmise is further supported by the use made of the linguist-stick at a court sitting. When the linguist is to pronounce judgment on behalf of the chief, he transfers his stick from his right to his left hand to leave the right hand free for gesticulation. He raises it about an inch from the ground, and ends the judgment with the following words, *Woamfa asɛm yi amma amma yɛamfa asopa antie, na wofaa abaa yi bɔɔ no a, na wodi aboa*, meaning that if the case had not been brought before the chief and his elders for their impartial hearing, and one of the litigants had struck the other with a stick, he would have dealt with the fallen as one does with a beast.

Top Two gilded staffs of office of linguists of the Ruler of the Sefwi State, Western Region. The top of one is in the form of a pineapple, that of the other is a three-headed man wearing a crown. The former symbolizes the saying that a pineapple should only be plucked when it is ripe, the latter that wise counsel comes from the head not only of one man but of several.

Foot The palanquin, *apakan*, of the Nsutahene, Ashanti. The sides are decorated with triangles of leopard skin and the circular ends with Maltese crosses, also of leopard skin. In Ashanti, apart from the Asantehene, only heads of Divisions are allowed such decorations on their palanquins. Inside is spread a *nsaa* blanket. There is a velvet cushion for a seat and a silk one for a back-rest. The poles through the loops on the sides are borne on the shoulders of four carriers.

The *adidie* or eating-place of the Nsutahene, Ashanti, with a circular dining-table in traditional style decorated with *mprengo* brass nails. The dish on it is of clay. At the side is an imported brass vessel containing a water jug and a stool with a carved lion as its *sɛkyɛdua* or column.

Two engraved brass vessels, *frowa*, used as containers for skin ointment or pomade. The ointment is extracted from the fruit of the shea butter tree. On a beautifully engraved brass tray are two ornate clay dishes, *ananane*, used in melting the shea butter or pomade before use. The articles are in the Prempeh II Jubilee Museum, Kumasi.

Top An elder of the council of the Ruler of the Akim Kotoku State, Eastern Region, smoking *taasɛn*, traditional pipes.

Centre Bronze oil lamps, *nkanea* or *atanea*, of the Asantehene together with their torches. A wick is floated in palm oil poured into the bowl at the top of the lamp.

Foot A *ware* board, carved in the shape of a stool, from the Prempeh II Jubilee Museum, Kumasi. *Ware* is a traditional game of the Akans with parallels found in other parts of Africa and is played by two people facing one another with the board between them. The game involves shifting about the four pebbles in each of the twelve cups. The larger cups at each end of the board are repositories for the pebbles won by the players in the course of the game.

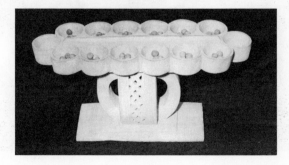

Top Wa Na's horse in ceremonial trappings with attendant.

Foot The Nayiri of Mamprusi in ceremonial robes holding the traditional *kpana* spear which he keeps in his own personal custody for self-protection.

CHAPTER SEVEN

Legacy of the Ghanaian Craftsman

'Panoply', which has been used in place of the word 'regalia' in the title of this book, literally means a full set of armour, the complete equipment required for the battlefield or some such encounter in life. It implies something that gives strength, power and confidence.

If what has been written has instead appeared to the reader as little more than a drab catalogue of some baubles of 'ancient' Ghana with explanatory notes, this is the inevitable result of the difficulty in trying to write about the creative minds of artists and craftsmen. The works of these artists, however, apart from their functional and aesthetic value, reflect the beliefs and values of the people and enshrine those sentiments which give them their mental and spiritual equilibrium. In this chapter an attempt is made to evaluate the social and artistic significance of Ghanaian regalia.

REGALIA AND THE PEOPLE'S SPIRITUAL FORTIFICATION

Chiefs, the custodians of the legacy of these artists and craftsmen, continue to exist, if in changed circumstances as far as the government of the country goes. One of the ways in which they make their influence still felt is the continuation of the observance of traditional festivals, great dramas which embrace all the arts of the people. A festival is an occasion not for the chief, his elders and attendants alone, but for all his subjects. The stools and swords or whatever the 'mercy seats' are, which are believed to be inhabited by the souls of ancestors, are cleansed for such a festival and thereby the whole chiefdom is also believed to have been cleansed of any defilements. The ancestors are fed with the first fruits of the fields or from the first catch, and prayers are offered to them or through them to the Supreme Deity: the *Onyame* of the Akans, the *Mawu* of the Ewes, the *Dzemawon* of the Gas and the *Nawuni* of the Dagombas in the north.

When the worship of the ancestors is finished, the chief, their living representative, sits in state with all the pomp and pageantry his regalia provide, to receive the homage of his people and in return to extend to them hospitality and bestow gifts. There is drumming and dancing, merriment and feasting. After the festivities the elders remain to confer on important affairs of state.

A Christian missionary facetiously dismissed the logic of belief in the ancestors and their cult with the remark that they were a very bold people who could sincerely believe that their deceased relations were such saints that they automatically upon death became intermediaries between the living and the Supreme Deity. This is, of course, one point of view, but it may be considered as an example of prejudice, which superficially makes a neat point, while obviously failing to consider the deeper significance or fundamental basis of a people's beliefs.

A book such as this is not the proper medium through which to pursue the logic or otherwise of a people's religion. But there is one point of interest and it is this: that the handiwork of the craftsman – the stool, the sword, the linguist-stick, or whatever it may be – helps, as a symbol, to give reality or intelligibility to what a people believe to be the explanation of life upon earth and life after death.

It is this explanation of the whole life – that is to say the life not interrupted or discontinued by death – which has provided Ghanaians, both as individuals and as ethnic groups, with that spiritual fortification which has enabled them so often to face the storms and stresses of life with equanimity.

REGALIA AS SYMBOLS OF AUTHORITY

One social function of regalia which must be the most obvious is their enhancement of the authority of the chief. The principal stool of the state, which enshrines the souls of the people, past, living and yet to be born, is his throne, and the constitutional question is sometimes posed: who is greater, the stool or the chief. At least the chief could say with Louis XIV of France, '*L'état, c'est moi*'.

At ceremonial gatherings the minstrels, horn-blowers, drummers and court-criers proclaim the military successes of his predecessors and remind the public and his enemies that he is the descendant of such a one, who killed and humbled such a one, and will not shrink, if necessary, from repeating the deeds of his forebears. Certain items of regalia could be possessed by subordinate chiefs only with the authority of their paramount chief. The powers betokened by the regalia of the Ghanaian king or paramount ruler are perhaps best summed up in one of the appellations

Two of the three ceremonial stools of the
Akroponghene, Ruler of the Akwapim State,
Eastern Region, seen in the stool-house at
Akropong. Here is other equipment the
ancestors will require when they enter: a
palanquin covered with *kente* cloth, a short
drum, a walking stick and a clay bowl for
water.

The Chief Priest of the Mafi State of Tongu,
Volta Region, sitting outside the temple under
his charge.

103

accorded the Asantehene, which means that it is he who removes the ring off the finger of a disobedient subject up through his shoulder.

Yet the paradox of the significance of the regalia to a chief is that they remind him of his responsibility to his people. If he smashes the egg of state by holding it too tight or too loose and is therefore removed from office, the stool-house will never see his black stool, no matter what good he may have done in the past, and his decorated sandals will be removed from his feet in public the moment he is deposed.

The regalia enhance not the chief as a person but the office which he holds. That is why the chief, on being destooled, may be allowed to retain any property, personal or real, that he may have acquired with his private funds during his reign, but not any contributions he may have made to the royal inheritance.

The supremacy of the people in the last resort is denoted by the symbolic top of one of the linguist-staffs of the Essumegyahene in Ashanti, called *apupuo a ɔbɔɔ n'asuo, ɔda nsukakye.* This represents a large fish lying in the middle of a stream with a number of small water-snails lying along the banks; the saying goes that the Creator first made the water-snails and put them in the stream; the fish came later and, because of its size, pushed itself to the centre.

REGALIA AS A GUIDE TO THE STUDY OF GHANAIAN SOCIETY

To the student of Ghanaian society and to the dilettante the regalia are of perennial interest. We have seen of what use they are in understanding the Ghanaian's search for spiritual contentment and in appraising the basis of the chief's authority. Similar benefits are to be found in a study of the people's general history and culture. In view, however, of the far-reaching social and cultural changes which are sweeping the country, we must examine more closely, with the help of our knowledge of the regalia, some aspects of the people's culture – their cosmology, religion, theory of the nature of man, and social values.

Professor K. A. Busia deals expertly with these subjects in his contribution to a volume of essays entitled *African Worlds* (Oxford University Press, 1954); and Mr J. H. Kwabena Nketia, a Ghanaian musicologist and associate professor at the University of Ghana, has made useful contributions to our knowledge of these matters with his studies of Ghanaian music

The pouring of a libation at the
stool-house of the Head of the Dome
or Adonten Division of the Anlo
State at Anloga, Volta Region.

The chair of state of a Dutch
governor of the then Gold Coast in
the eighteenth century. It is in the
Ghana National Museum, Accra.

The Palace of the Anumhene, Eastern Region, built in 1723. In contrast to the Wa Na's Palace in the north, the design is influenced by the European-built castles and forts on the coast. In the foreground is the foundation stone, believed to make anyone who touches it swell. It is called Ɔbosommoɔ, the Devil's Stone.

in several monographs and articles. I acknowledge my indebtedness for the enlightenment I have received from their work. For the benefit of readers to whom some of the terms used in this kind of study are strange, some definitions are called for.

Briefly stated, cosmology means knowledge or ideas about creation and the universe. Religion refers to how people attune themselves to this knowledge or these ideas through a system of faith, worship, personal attitudes and behaviour. The theory of the nature of man is the explanation of how the different natures of man – mind, spirit or soul, and body – came about and how they harmonize into one single being. By social values is meant the yardstick or standard by which a people judge between what is right or wrong, good or bad.

COSMOLOGY

The Ghanaian traditional belief, generally speaking, is that the universe, the world of spirits and of all living beings and things, was created by a Supreme Deity, who also created Himself, the First, the Elder of the vast world – *asase terε, na Onyame ne panin.* This is acknowledged by the drummer of the talking drums in the opening stanza of the drum's repertoire: *Asase gye nsa nom; abayifoɔ monnye nsa nom; Onyankopɔn, Tweaduampɔn, Bɔnyame, gye nsa nom.* (Earth, take your rum and drink; witches, take your rum and drink; O Dependable One [one of the names given to the Supreme Deity], Creator of God, take your rum and drink.)

This Supreme Deity was anthropomorphic, he had the form or personality of a man and once lived close to mankind, on the rooftops. A story in Akan mythology tells how he reached the skies. He was inadvertently given a jolt with a pestle by an old woman pounding palm kernels in a mortar. The more jolts he received, the higher he ascended, until at last he reached the high heavens and decided to remain there.

RELIGION

The Supreme Being now being so far away, it became necessary to have intermediaries between him and man. Therefore, those of his creations which were regarded animistically as having living souls, and which appeared to touch the heavens or the horizon, were given messages or offerings to take to the Sky God. Such 'messengers' included trees, rivers, lakes and seas.

Here, it is suggested, lies the origin of the worship of lesser gods (*abosom*), sharing the same status as the ancestors who on death joined the Supreme Being in his heavenly abode and shared his divinity.

Certain animals and the earth itself were also regarded as sacred.

The role of the Tree of God, the altar created for the Supreme Deity, is reminiscent of the role of the lesser deities. It is represented in the regalia of chiefs by the ornamental Tree of God against which the Asantehene leans in his moments of distress, sitting only on cushions laid on the ground instead of on a stool or chair.

The lesser deities also have the power to bless or to do harm to man; that is why a drummer would offer a prayer of propitiation to the tree or trees out of which the component parts of his drum were made.

The depth of the people's sense of gratitude for the blessings received from some of these lesser deities is to be seen from the following stanza of the recitations of the *durugya* flute of the Asantehene:

> *Adutwum Nsuo yɛdware nom,*
> *Ɛnna yɛasa na yɛasane de asi ntoma;*
> *Asante Kɔtɔkɔ, yɛn mma ne yɛn na.*
> *Yɛanhyia wo a anka yɛbɛyɛ dɛn?*
> *Sakyiakwa Asuo Abenaa,*
> *Adutwum Nsuo Amponkuru,*
> *Asante Kɔtɔkɔ yɛfua tadua hunu,*
> *Agyan nna so.*
> *Akumanini, Dammirifa.*

> River Adutwum, in you we bathe and from you we
> have our drink,
> From you we collect the water to wash our clothes.
> *Asante Kɔtɔkɔ,* our children and grandchildren,
> But for you what would we have done?
> Sakyiakwa River, lady born on Tuesday,
> River Adutwum Amponkuru,
> *Asante Kɔtɔkɔ,* we carry a catapult without a dart;
> a bow without an arrow.
> Mighty one, condolences.

In addition to the lesser deities and the ancestors there were impersonal magical forces called *asuman*, minor deities residing in beads, charms or

Priest and priestesses outside one of the temples of the three gods of the Gbugla State at Prampram, Accra District. The gods are Laloi, Osabu and Digble.

The senior wife of the Ya Na, Northern Region, holding her staff of office, *tangbee*, together with her maid carrying her personal belongings in an enamel pan wrapped in a net, *kpanjogu*.

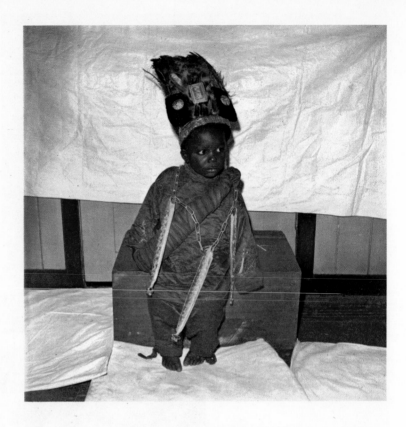

The Ɔkra are representative of the soul of the Ruler of the Akim Abuakwa State, Eastern Region, in ceremonial robes. It is an accepted fiction among some of the Akans that the soul of the Ruler inhabits a younger courtier who then becomes identified with him and accompanies him on ceremonial parades and on the battlefield. This is related to the other belief that the spirit of a deceased person may enter a living person through whom he may speak, particularly of the manner of his death if it is suspected that he had been bewitched.

The band across his shoulder is stuffed with charms and his necklace is a gold chain with gold gongs. The hat is of eagle feathers with embossed gold decorations. On the battlefield the Ɔkra would wear the same uniform as the Ruler and would ring his steel gongs to announce the approach of his master. If the Ruler out of fear deadened the sound of the gongs with leaves, this was taken as deserting his men and he would be shot immediately.

Left The Parliamentary Mace incorporating traditional motifs.

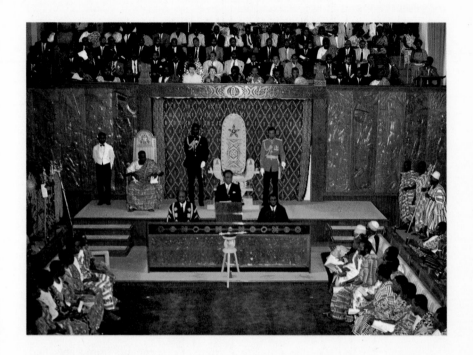

Opening of Parliament by Osagyefo Dr Kwame Nkrumah, President of the Republic of Ghana. Behind him is the Presidential Throne in the form of a traditional stool.

talismans. They received their power from the lesser deities and acted in obedience to certain formulae. Several instances have been given of representations of these *asuman* being used to decorate stools, chairs or robes, or being worn as bracelets or headgear for protection and for driving away evil spirits. It has been stated elsewhere that the use of these *asuman* may have come from the people's association with the Islamic faith, as some of them contain inscriptions taken from the Koran. There was, further, a belief in the magical powers of witches, *abayifoɔ*, and certain forest creatures, such as the Little Folk, *Mmoatia*, and the Forest Monster, *Sasabonsam*. These, particularly *Sasabonsam*, are used as models for gold-weights.

NATURE OF MAN

As regards the nature of man, the Akan theory, which is fairly representative of the whole of Ghana, is that man is both a corporeal and a spiritual being. He inherits his corporeal nature, that is, his physical being, from his mother, and this is called his *mogya* or blood. It is this biological or 'blood' association that determines his lineage and clan, his links with successive generations and his rights and obligations as a citizen, such as allegiance and rights of tenure. A distinction is made between lineage and clan which is as follows:

A lineage may be defined as a unilateral group of descendants from a specified ancestor or ancestress. Members of the clan are descendants from a common remote ancestor or ancestress, not specified as in the case of a lineage, and are bound together by respect for common totemic and other taboos, *akyiwadeɛ*. Whereas members of a lineage are as a rule domiciled in the same village or locality, members of a clan are scattered throughout the country and belong to different political units. Membership of a clan does not therefore determine citizenship.

The spiritual being of man is made up of his personality or 'ego', *sunsum*, and his soul or life force, *kra*, both of which are derived from his father. The *sunsum* determines his *ntɔn*. The *ntɔn* is a patrilineal grouping and is embraced by a spirit, a particle of which a man inherits from his father. The *kra* or soul is regarded as a small bit of the Creator that lives in every person. It is bestowed by the Creator through the child's father and it returns to Him after death. A euphemistic way of announcing death is: *Ɔkɔ ne kra akyi.* (His soul is gone whence it came.)

A traditional ruler of the Shai area in the Eastern Region dressed in an appliqué-worked cloth and with a necklace of several strings of precious beads. Swearing allegiance to him is one of the elders wearing a magnificent imported brocade.

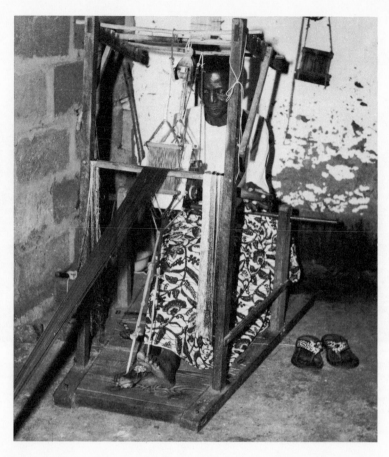

A weaver of Anloga, Volta Region, at work on his loom. He is Bernard Akor Ahorlu, one of the craftsmen who represented Ghana (then Gold Coast) at the British Empire Exhibition of 1925 at Wembley, London. In the foreground is a mounted warp of threads used for *kente* cloth.

Both the *sunsum* and the *kra* of rulers are fed, purified and worshipped in practically the same manner as the spirits of their ancestors, dwelling in the black stools; but in this instance the media of worship are respectively the *abosomfena* and the *akrafena*.

Belief in the spiritual nature of man is also to be seen in child-naming, puberty and funeral rites.

SOCIAL VALUES

The people's social values can almost be guessed from what has been said about their concept of the nature of the universe and their beliefs regarding the twofold nature of man and the continuity of life even after death. The Ghanaian is a citizen of an undivided community of the dead, the living and the yet to be born; and, as the Akans say, he must do nothing that will bring disgrace to him as a member of this community, *animguasɛ mfata kanniba*. All this is, of course, largely a theological and abstract concept, and the reader is entitled to know what it amounts to in its practical application to the business of everyday living.

At the outset, then, it should be clearly understood that the State of Ghana is not theocratic. It has all the trappings and paraphernalia of civil authority. Civil laws are made and infringement of them is actionable in the courts, which, if one makes allowances for bad judgments, are far from what a schoolboy howler described as a place where justice was dispensed with!

But the ruler and his elders, who also constitute some of the courts, realize that in the performance of their duties they are acting as representatives of the ancestors and of posterity; and the people they rule and judge are co-citizens of this tripartite world. The citizen accepts his civic responsibilities and subjection to the law in the same spirit.

Both the ruler and the ruled are aware that the ancestors have an interest in what happens on earth, and they have no doubt that these ancestors will apply their own sanctions if they are given cause to do so.

We have not, however, discussed how the people distinguish in their legal system, moral behaviour and general social relations between good and bad, right and wrong. In other words, what constitutes disgrace for the *kanniba* and his community? This question is partly answered by the fact that Ghanaians accept certain acts as being naturally good or bad. Moreover, the ancestors have handed down a code of laws to govern legal and moral judgment which has been modified and augmented by succeeding generations. It is significant that in Ashanti this code of laws was said to have been read out to the people for the first time by Kɔmfo Anɔkye, the chief priest who conjured the Golden Stool from the skies, at the assembly during which the stool descended. Presumably this was to give the laws the force of sanctity.

The reason for this discussion of social values in a book about royal regalia is that many of the sayings already referred to as being symbolically represented on gold-weights, on the tops of umbrellas and linguist-staffs and in the names of textiles, jewellery and designs, allude to this inherited code of laws, which covers every field of human and social relations. A few examples will not be out of place.

Actionable behaviour under customary law

i. Tracing someone's pedigree with a view to slighting him.
ii. Insulting or assaulting a chief or functionary of the state; conversely, a chief losing his temper to the extent of laying hands on a subject.
iii. Swearing an oath on an inanimate object or on a woman in her menstrual period, since these are unable to appear before the chief and his court to reply to the oath. (Swearing an oath referring to some national calamity in the history of the state is the procedure for seeking to initiate court proceedings.)
iv. Making love to a woman whose adolescence has not been publicly proclaimed through the puberty rite; or making love in the bush or in public.

Rules of moral behaviour contained in proverbs and sayings

(Vernacular versions are given.)

i. *Respect for old age and authority.*

a. If you are as tall as or taller than your father, you are still not his equal – *Wo sene w'agya tentene a, ɛnyɛ wo tipɛn ne no.*
b. If you wish someone senior or more knowledgeable than yourself to identify a bird, you do not first yourself remove the bird's feathers – *Obi ntutu anoma ho nkɔkyerɛ panin.*

ii. *Reward comes only to the deserving.*

a. When a child learns to wash his hands before a meal, he dines with his elders – *Abɔfra hunu ne nsa hohoro a, ɔne mpanimfoɔ didi.*
b. If a child laments at a funeral like a grown-up, he is given a white kola-nut (kola-nuts are chewed by mourners to kill hunger and the white are more costly than the red) – *Abɔfra su panin su a, yɛma no besehene.*

116

iii. *Selfishness does not pay.*

a. If you alone drink a medicine for long life or a cure against death, you will be left alone in the waste land – *Ɔbaakofoɔ di ɛkyerɛ aduro a, ɔkyɛre amanfo so.*

b. If you do not allow a friend to get a nine, you will never yourself get a ten – *Woamma wo yɔnko antwa nkoron a, wonnya edu ntwa.*

iv. *Obstinacy is to be avoided.*

a. If a friend who has asked you to accompany him somewhere says you should return, you do not argue with him – *Dee ɔse ma yɛnkɔ se ma yɛnsane a yɛnnye no akyinnye.*

b. If you touch shrubs and they turn into a forest, you have to turn back – *Sɛ wokɔka mfofo na sɛ ɛdane kwaeɛ a, na ɛsɛsɛ wosane ara.*

REGALIA AS WORKS OF ART

Kenneth Young, reviewing Sir Herbert Read's *The Forms of Things Unknown*, considers that he over-stresses the function of art as creating objects the perception of which leads to new knowledge.

He believes that a work of art, by dipping into the irrationality of man which is part of the whole inexplicable rationality of the universe, is at once a means of integrating the personality and of discovering, in the Shakespearean words of his title, the forms of things unknown.

. . . Is Sir Herbert not really asking art to bear too heavy a burden? I hope his next book will be a plea for teaching us how to pray.

Daily Telegraph, 5 August 1960.

Similarly this book, particularly the present chapter on the legacy of the Ghanaian craftsman, may be criticized for laying undue stress on the regalia of chiefs as a reflection of Ghanaian society. But that the various items of Ghanaian regalia *are* a mirror to society is, I hope, proved. For they *do* reflect – as does the work of artists in other lands – the society by which they were inspired.

Be that as it may, the regalia are, first and foremost, works of art and this fact requires emphasis in our appraisal. It is fashionable in books on art to draw a distinction between the fine arts and the useful arts, the distinction depending on whether the works in question were made principally to give pleasure, in which case they belong to the first category, or qualify for the latter group. The tendency has been to regard all African traditional art-works as belonging to the latter category because, it is alleged, they are invariably used for domestic or ritual purposes. It is, however, a debatable point whether, for example, the craftsmen responsible for the Ashanti gold-weights inscribed with proverbs were more concerned with providing counter-balances for the weighing of gold dust or with giving expression to some thoughts about the world around them and about a life which had roused their emotions.

Whether they produce *useful* works or works to give *aesthetic delight*, African craftsmen are also properly regarded as artists, and their creations as works of art. I hope that the descriptions given and photographs shown of some of their chiefs' regalia will be accepted as ample proof.

It is now intended to refer briefly to the Ghanaian artist-craftsman's approach to art. It must, however, be observed at the outset that traditional Ghanaian craftsmen were most skilled in ornamental art and the connoisseur of African art will perhaps be disappointed not to find anything in their sculpture to match the celebrated Ife bronze heads and the fantastic range of masks and human and animal wooden figures from the Congo.

According to the Akans, craftsmen and musicians are the linguists or spokesmen of the Supreme Deity, the Creator of the universe, of man and of all things – *ɔdomankoma akyerɛma*. They are thus interpreters of the eternal truths of creation and of the joys, sorrows, needs and destinies of man. In the execution of their task they show every quality that by universal consent is associated with the artist: originality, imagination, feeling, skill, a sense of beauty and, one might add, a sense of humour. One of the many examples one could give of these qualities of the Ghanaian artist-craftsman is a portrayal of the inscrutable nature of the Supreme Deity. To effect this, the designer of this particular gold-weight has made two figures lying upon the ground, the one face up and the other face down. The first, with his face to the skies, is in effect asking the second, 'If I, with my face turned up, cannot see the Sky God, what chance have you of seeing him?'

The *ɔkyeame*, linguist or spokesman, is regarded as a wise man; and, according to an Akan proverb, wise men speak and are spoken to not in ordinary language but in proverbs: *ɔba nyansafoɔ yɛbu no bɛ yɛnka no asɛm*. In court the linguist will listen to the case of the litigant and in turn will present the case to the chief and his elders in court language. It is said that it is only the bad or inefficient linguist who fails to recast the language of the litigant and simply tells the court members, 'You must have heard what the litigant has had to say.' An analogy with the linguist's approach to his task in the court, perhaps, explains the Ghanaian artist's partiality for

A durbar procession of a ruler under an *akomponkyiniɛ* umbrella with his linguists carrying their staffs of office.

Sir Charles Noble Arden-Clarke, first Governor-General of Ghana, being welcomed to a durbar.

119

abstract and stylized forms and the almost complete absence of naturalistic design. Two adjoining spirals represent the horns of a ram; and just as the linguist in court in presenting the litigant's case will mention only the salient points made, so the carver of a *baduaba* fertility doll concerns himself only with the flat head, slender nose, conspicuous eyelashes, thin lips and protruding breasts and navel.

No greater tribute could have been paid to these spokesmen of the Supreme Deity and of Ghanaian society than the fact that their countrymen are finding in their legacy a source of inspiration, as is seen, for example, in the use made of traditional music at state functions and in the designing of the parliamentary regalia of Independent and Republican Ghana.